INTARSIA
30 PATTERNS
FOR THE SCROLLSAW

INTARSIA
30 PATTERNS
FOR THE SCROLLSAW

John Everett

GUILD OF MASTER CRAFTSMAN PUBLICATIONS

First published 2001 by
Guild of Master Craftsman Publications Ltd,
166 High Street, Lewes,
East Sussex, BN7 1XN

Text, project templates and step-by-step photographs
© John Everett 2001
© in the Work GMC Publications Ltd
Cover and finished project photography by Chris Skarbon

ISBN 1 86108 212 6

A catalogue record of this book is available from the
British Library.

Cover design by Richard Peters, GMC Publications Studio
Book design by Phil and Traci Morash, Fineline Studios

Typeface: Officina Sans

Colour origination by Viscan Graphics (Singapore)

Printed in Hong Kong by H & Y Printing Ltd

Measurements

Throughout this book instances may be found where a metric measurement has fractionally varying imperial equivalents, usually within $\frac{1}{16}$in either way. This is because in each particular case the closest imperial equivalent has been given.

A mixture of metric and imperial measurements should NEVER be used – always use one or the other.

See also metric conversion table on page 115.

Contents

PROJECTS

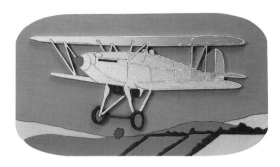

Introduction

Intarsia is an attractive and innovative way to make decorative and functional items in wood and other materials. Part of its appeal lies in the extra dimension it offers to the otherwise flat surface of your selected material; the cut creates a shadow which casts across the individual elements of the piece. It's a bit like painting by numbers, with the outlines for blocks of colour ready-made for you to paint in. With intarsia, a sheet of wood or alternative material, is covered with a cutting pattern, and the component parts are individually cut out, shaped and finished off before being recombined to make the design complete.

This book shows you how to make simple, traditional designs, but also more original and sophisticated collages and three-dimensional projects. Some use the intarsia patterns as one part of a larger project to which other features might be added – a mirror or hooks for a coat rack, for example. Once you have completed one or two of the simpler projects, you will find intarsia a great effect for styling attractive scrollsaw projects for the home – providing, of course, that you take care and do not rush your work, which can lead to mistakes.

You need very few basic pieces of equipment to make all the projects in this book (and I outline these more fully in the Materials and equipment section that follows), but fundamentally you need a scrollsaw and a basic minidrill outfit, both of which are widely available. Indeed, many craftspeople and hobbyists will already have these items in their workshop.

I have designed the patterns for this book to cater for a range of skill levels – from the straightforward to the more elaborate designs, in a wide variety of subjects – so that, hopefully, there is something here for everyone. The projects are organized by their form and function, and then in order of relative complexity, but one's view of this will vary a little depending on individual scrollsawing experience. Apply a flexible approach, using the order given here as a guideline and, if something appeals to you, give it a try.

For the beginner, though, it is best to start off with one or two of the simpler projects to get a feel for intarsia; it is relatively easy to tackle any of the patterns once you are comfortable with these. The main requirement is a little patience; take your time and concentrate on accuracy rather than speed. You will find that as you progress, your proficiency and speed will naturally follow. Ultimately, though, the whole idea is to enjoy your work and achieve a good result, so how fast you complete it is far less important.

Once you have some confidence in your work, don't be afraid to experiment with alternative woods or materials. For example, the mirror frame project makes use of a Celtic knotwork pattern cut from a thickish sheet of brass, which is a little different. Equally, of course, this design would work well in a light-coloured wood, too. You might also like to lift elements of a design and apply it to other decorative items for the home.

Many designs can be completed either as pictures in frames, wall plaques or used as a decorative motif for something else – a cabinet, perhaps, or a piece of furniture. Where projects need to be affixed to a backing panel, I have not provided a special template as this is really down to preference and may be dictated by your chosen frame. Similarly, you may prefer to select your own finish for your designs. A wide variety of attractive finishes and treatments are offered by the patterns in this book to give you the inspiration to be bold.

The idea is to remain flexible and consider alternatives if you think they work well. You can afford to be a little adventurous, keeping in mind the practical application and the integrity of the work.

I hope you have lots of fun with these new patterns – enjoy!

Materials

Various materials can be used on the scrollsaw, and the minidrill. Wood and wood-based man-made sheet materials are, of course, the most obvious and these are used most frequently for scrollsaw projects. They include hard- and softwoods, ply in all its variations and MDF (medium density fibreboard), which is now readily available in a wide variety of thicknesses and grades.

Hardwood

Some hardwoods, such as oak, may have been fully cured some years prior to being used, so will have become extremely hard indeed. In this case, it would be better to use a metal-cutting blade rather than a standard variety.

Softwood

Some pines and hemlocks are so soft that they leave a fibrous finish once sawn. So bear in mind that with these types of timber, careful sanding, particularly on the cut edges, may be required to get a smooth finish.

Man-made boards

Birch ply
Good quality birch ply is the best to use for intarsia work as it splinters less and the clean, creamy surface will take a number of different finishes well, including watercolour paint.

MDF
This is a very versatile product. As with chipboard and other particle boards, fixing screws can be a problem, but this can often

A selection of natural and man-made woods. From the bottom up: oak, mahogany, pine board, MDF and plywood

be overcome by using two different fixing methods, for example glue and screws, glue and pins or, indeed, by arranging things so that the fixings pass through the MDF and are secured into parts made from regular timber.

One of the advantages of MDF is the clean edge left on the material after cutting which means that, generally, MDF doesn't require any sanding, other than the cleaning of saw tearout. This is a tremendous advantage when cutting intricate and detailed work, which is almost impossible to sand. In addition, the face sides of MDF boards provide an adequate surface which does not need sanding and, as with other sheet material of this sort, has no grain, and will cut easily at the same speed in any direction.

Remember, however, that MDF can be toxic when inhaled and it is essential to take safety precautions (please refer to 'The dangers of sawdust', page 11).

A typical scrollsaw

Equipment

To make up the projects in this book, you really need very few pieces of equipment, primarily the scrollsaw, the minidrill and a few key accessories. As this is a pattern book, providing inspiring ideas for using this equipment, I assume the reader is already sufficiently familiar with the tools to make a start. Keeping the beginner to intarsia in mind, however, there are a few helpful pointers for using the scrollsaw and minidrill.

The scrollsaw

It is the task of the scrollsaw to cut the individual parts of the final design and, in terms of the throat depth required, the projects in this book have been designed to accommodate virtually any size scrollsaw.

Blades

To an extent, the size and type of blade you use for your scrollsaw depends upon your chosen material. Most of the patterns in this book involve tight radius turns which require a small gauge number blade, a size 5 or less. Most types of intarsia panel include some very small pieces. For this, a size 3 or smaller scrollsaw blade is required.

If you want to cut into either MDF or ply, you need a skip–tooth blade, whereas real woods require a standard blade. For plywood, use a reverse–tooth blade to avoid splintering. With this type of blade, the bottom few teeth work in the opposite direction to the main teeth and the blade cuts into the wood, thereby eliminating tearing.

If you intend cutting pieces from brass or other metals, then you need one or possibly two metal-cutting blades. When you use metal-cutting blades, keep in mind that a slow cutting speed is essential; blades have a tendency to break easily.

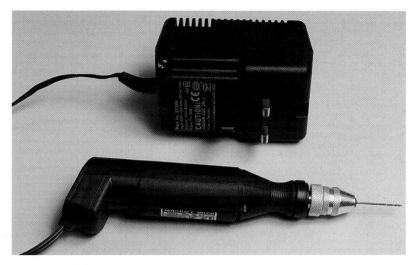

The basic minidrill with power adaptor

Accessory table

For cutting out very small parts with the scrollsaw, another essential piece of equipment is an accessory table to prevent the smallest parts falling away from the stock material through the blade hole and onto the floor!

To make an accessory table, all you need is a thin piece of sheet material, MDF or ply for example, approximately 3–6mm (⅛–¼in) thick, which you clamp securely into position on top of your existing saw table. Run the saw blade into the centre of the sheet prior to clamping it into position and this will prevent losing even the smallest of cut outs through the hole of the blade.

The minidrill

Most minidrill owners will already have the basic hobby kit. This kit usually consists of the basic drill, a power unit to enable the drill to use mains electricity directly and an assortment of accessories which can be used with the drill.

Minidrill accessories

The most useful accessory for the minidrill is a miniature drum sander attachment (available for all types of this tool) which comes complete with replacement sanding sleeves in a variety of grades.

For shaping operations, it is also useful to have a few burrs for getting into the smallest of radii.

Bench clamp

A bench clamp is also useful for carrying out sanding and shaping operations, leaving both hands free for better control of the work piece. As many people do not have a bench clamp for their minidrills (and some types of drill do not carry such an accessory within their range anyway), you can make a bench clamp for your own drill in your workshop at minimum cost. (Please see the photograph on the following page for a working arrangement that I find helpful.)

Using bench clamps offers you better control of the work piece

Flat-nosed pliers

A pair of flat-nosed pliers is of real benefit when using the mindrill – and I speak from experience – to stop yourself from gradually grinding away your fingernails during the sanding and shaping operations!

Flexible sanding pad

You will find a flexible sanding pad a useful accessory for small intarsia items. It forms itself around curves and sands into small corners with ease.

Alternatively, a miniature file will get into the smallest of places and can be used to clean up the remaining tight corners.

Extras

There are a number of additional materials and pieces of equipment, which you might already have in your workroom. These include:

Spray Mount
Jigsaw (optional)
Pillar drill (optional)
Corner clamps
Various grades of sandpaper
Range of paints, from enamel to watercolour
Paint primer
Glues, including wood glue and epoxy resin
    and adhesives such as Araldite

A range of enamel paints

Scrollsaw basics

Scaling a pattern up or down

You can do this on a photocopier, or you can scale up the template using a grid. If the grid pattern is based on a 1cm grid (as it is in this book) and you want to create a 200% enlargement, you need to copy the template shape onto a 2cm grid.

If you number the rows of grids on both the original and the copy, it will be easier to find your place quickly.

Put a dot at each point where the cutting line crosses from one square to another. All you then have to do is join the dots, ensuring any curves follow the line of the original.

Sketch in the design first with a light pencil, to ensure you get the drawing exactly right before you commit to an ink line.

Take your time making a satisfactory cutting pattern, as the quality of the finished item will depend on the accuracy of this template.

Attaching a cutting pattern

Once you begin to cut out and make up intarsia patterns, you will quickly appreciate an additional copy of your cutting pattern. For all but the simplest of designs, the spare pattern is useful for laying out each part as it is cut in sequence. This eliminates repeatedly working out where each piece fits, particularly when the pattern you are working has a

A good cutting pattern is essential for intarsia work

number of similarly shaped pieces. Having an extra copy made at your local copy shop will save hours of frustrating puzzle-solving.

Attach the cutting pattern using an adhesive – such as Spray Mount – or other low-tack adhesive. This will allow the rest of the cutting pattern to be easily removed from the blank once cutting has been completed.

With a little practice you will get the hang of using spray adhesive and find it easy to apply. Just remember that if you use too much adhesive when sticking the pattern to the blank, removing the pattern will prove messy, while too little adhesive will mean that the pattern won't stick properly.

Making a blank

A blank is a plainly cut piece of wood or other material. It is generally cut a little larger than the size of the cutting pattern, so that there is enough spare material for you to grip to successfully control the direction of the cut.

To make the blank, select the material you intend to use and place the cutting pattern on it so that it does not waste too much material. Draw around the outside of the cutting pattern – not too closely – so that the marked area is a little larger than the template. Cut the blank free from its sheet with a saw. A jigsaw is useful for this if you have one, but any other suitable saw will do just as well. Finally, sand off the edges of the material so that there is no saw tearout.

Setting up the scrollsaw

Before you start, make sure your scrollsaw is set up properly. It is important to check that it is firmly bolted to the bench, and that the

cables and plug are not damaged in any way, such as nicks and scratches in the insulation.

Some scrollsaws have an optional stand. This is a useful facility as it prevents your workbench space being taken up with tools and equipment. Some stands also have a built-in swivel chair for the operator. Whatever arrangement you have, make sure you are comfortable and relaxed.

The hold-down device helps to keep the workpiece flat on the table, preventing 'chattering' when you turn corners with the saw. Make sure you set the hold-down device correctly before starting to saw.

The tension of the blade must be adjusted before you begin sawing. If the blade is too tight, there is a risk of breakage, too loose and the sawing line could become inaccurate. See the manufacturer's manual for details of how to adjust the tension on your saw.

Basic cutting

Cutting with the scrollsaw is simple and you'll find you improve with practice. Keep your eye on the point where the saw blade meets the cutting line and just follow the line. After a while you will be able to cut perfect straight lines and gentle curves, as well as tight turns.

Stack sawing

Two or more identical pieces can be cut by a process known as stack sawing. Two or more blanks are simply fixed together (usually with double-sided adhesive tape) and sawn around at the same time. This makes the job easier to complete, and ensures that all the pieces are identical.

Just cut out the required number of blanks and stick them together with little pieces of double-sided adhesive tape on the waste side of the cutting line. Attach the cutting pattern to the top of the blank, and cut around the cutting pattern. You may find that the blade cuts slightly slower because of the thickness of the material, but try not to force the material into the blade.

Internal cutouts

An internal cutout is a part of a pattern that needs to be cut away, but does not meet any of the edges. The cutout often forms part of the ornamentation of the piece.

To make an internal cutout, you will need to drill a hole for the saw blade to pass through. If small, delicate cutouts are required, then you will need to use a drill bit only slightly larger than the width of your blade. If the cutout is not delicate, use a large drill bit, to make threading the saw blades easier. Put a scrap of wood behind the hole position when you drill so that you leave a clean edge at the back of the hole. This is particularly important if you are using plywood, as the splintering that can occur could spoil the final piece. Try to drill the starter holes near a sharp point or angle on the design. This will make it easier to ensure that the beginning and end of the cut meet up easily. If you were to begin your cutting line along a straight or gently curving section of the pattern, the start and finish of the cut might not meet exactly, making intricate filing or sanding necessary to make the cutting line meet precisely.

Secure the blade in the saw's bottom blade holder first. Thread the blade through your starter hole, secure the blade in the top blade holder and tension it properly. Check the manufacturer's handbook for the particular tensioning arrangement for your saw.

It is usually better to complete the internal cutouts first. This will ensure that there is enough waste material to grip when guiding the blank along the cutting line.

Finishing

There are many possible wood finishes but, for the projects in this book, we need only concern ourselves with paint finishes, enamels, wood stains and varnishes. All of these are available in a range of colours and shades.

Painting an undercoat

Whatever type of paint you are using, most woods, natural or artificial, will require some form of undercoat in order to get the best finish. The use of a primer is not only an advantage, but in the case of some artificial materials such as MDF, virtually essential to obtain an even coverage of paint. A white primer not only seals the wood prior to painting, so that the wood does not absorb too much paint, it also provides a degree of light reflection through the top coat of paint, giving the colour coat a brighter appearance.

Another advantage of using primer, particularly with softwoods and MDF, is that it renders immobile, and therefore removable with sandpaper, those annoying little bits that need to be sanded off but cannot be removed by sandpaper while the wood is bare.

Always allow the primer to dry thoroughly before attempting any further work on the piece. Acrylic primer usually only takes an hour to dry. Once fully dry, use fine sandpaper to get the surface smooth, ready for the top coat of paint.

Safety

Common sense

The most important thing to remember is to use your common sense. The blades used in the scrollsaw are thin with tiny teeth, and these teeth are capable of cutting through thick, hard materials. It therefore follows that, small though the teeth are, they are also capable of cutting through a finger or thumb. It is essential to keep an eye on where your fingers are in relation to the saw blade you are using.

Blade breakage

Most scrollsaw accidents occur when a scrollsaw-user applies too much pressure to the workpiece, in an endeavour to cut faster, and the blade breaks. Blades for the scrollsaw are not expensive so, if you find you need pressure to make the blade cut through your workpiece, change the blade. A replacement blade is considerably cheaper than a week or two off work with a damaged finger.

Protecting your eyes

It is important to wear safety goggles at all times when cutting unfamiliar materials, particularly when working metals. It may be a nuisance wearing them, but remember the slight inconvenience is nothing compared to the prospect of living with permanently damaged eyes. There are so many brands and type of goggles/safety glasses available cheaply, that it is well worth trying a few, to see which suits you best.

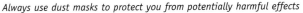

Always use dust masks to protect you from potentially harmful effects

The dangers of sawdust

The scrollsaw produces very fine sawdust which can remain suspended in the air for quite some time. This can be a particular problem to those who suffer from asthma and other respiratory tract problems. In addition, some materials, including a few hardwoods and some man-made sheet materials such as MDF, produce toxic dust (although there is now a formaldehyde-free range of MDF).

The importance of dust masks

Many scrollsaws have a dust extraction facility underneath the saw table; this is helpful but unfortunately not the complete answer, as there will always be dust produced above the saw table. To counteract this, most saws also have an air blower to keep the line on your cutting pattern free of sawdust, but this blows the ultra-fine dust into the air around you. Because of this, a dust mask must always be worn when cutting with the scrollsaw. There are many dust masks available in DIY stores and garages, so spend a little time finding one that you find comfortable to wear. Preventing damage is, after all, better than cure.

Cleaning up

Never use a dustpan and brush to clean up after cutting with your scrollsaw – it will simply spread the dust. Always vacuum up as much dust as possible. A build-up of fine dust can clog the working parts of your scrollsaw and, by applying good housekeeping rules, you can prevent such problems from occurring too often.

Projects

Floral clock

With the addition of a standard quartz clock movement, this little decorative wall clock will not only look good but keep perfect time, too.

For the clock's back panel and the flower overlay and numerals, select an appropriate material approximately 6mm (¼in) thick. I used MDF here, but ply will do just as well, although birch ply is best. Whichever material you choose, cut it with a reverse-tooth blade to avoid splintering. This is the key problem with cutting; after all, you want to maintain a neat edge on the numerals and petals, so do keep it in mind.

Make up your cutting patterns and stick them down onto your MDF or ply. First take the flower pattern as this encapsulates the clock movement. Drill an 8mm (⁵⁄₁₆in) hole (if your movement is the same size given here), or to fit your own, as long as it is large enough to fit the spindle. If you have one, a pillar drill will make your vertical hole easy work, but if not, try to keep whatever drill

you use as upright as possible. Take your time if drilling by hand so that the hands of the clock do not run out of true.

Now cut out the various parts for the clock and shape them using your minidrill with the drum sander attachment.

To assemble the clock, stick down the decorated numerals first and then add the floral overlay. Use the same drill to butt up the petals as you assemble the flower so that you have a perfect alignment for the clock spindle when you withdraw the drill bit.

Finally, fit your clock movement and hang your clock on the wall. Most of the readily available clock movements already have an attachment for hanging your piece to the wall moulded to their casing so, most likely, you will not need to attach one of your own.

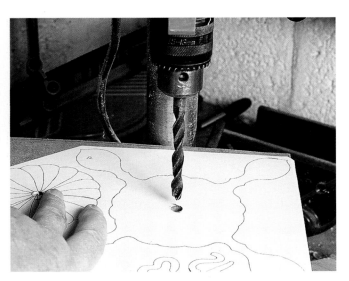

Using a pillar drill to make a clean spindle hole for the clock movement

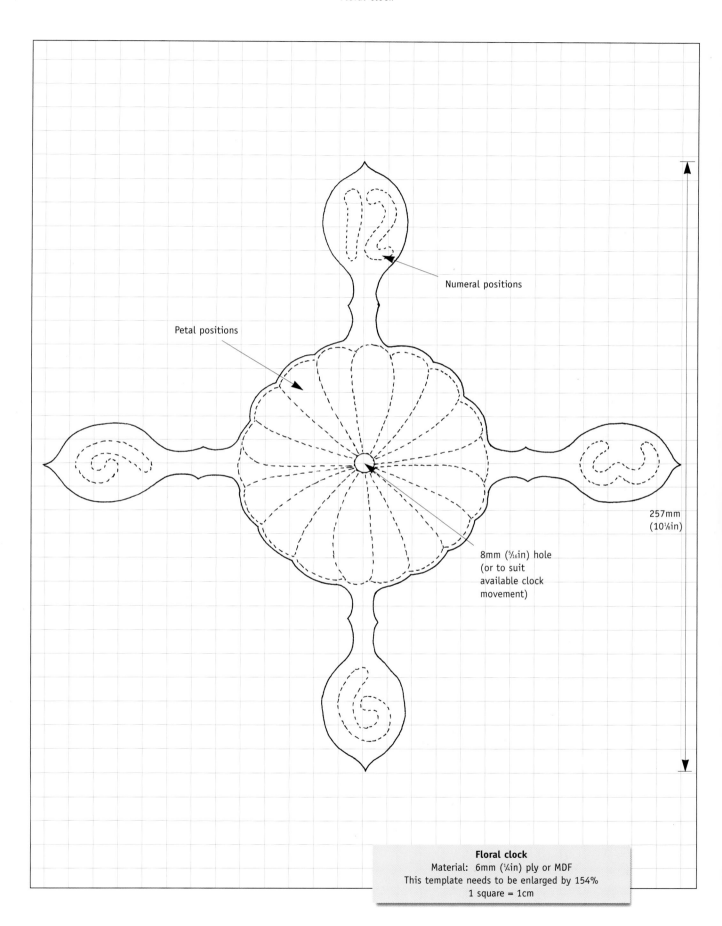

Numeral positions

Petal positions

257mm
(10⅛in)

8mm (⁵⁄₁₆in) hole
(or to suit
available clock
movement)

Floral clock
Material: 6mm (¼in) ply or MDF
This template needs to be enlarged by 154%
1 square = 1cm

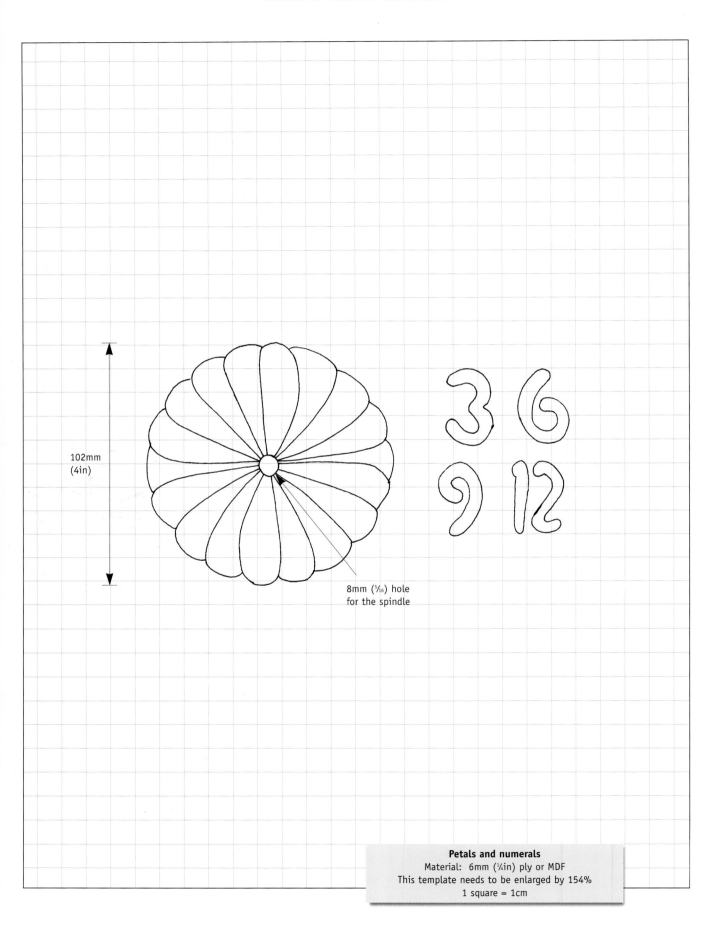

102mm
(4in)

8mm (⁵⁄₁₆) hole
for the spindle

Petals and numerals
Material: 6mm (¼in) ply or MDF
This template needs to be enlarged by 154%
1 square = 1cm

Floral mug rest

This is a fairly straightforward design, influenced by a classic floral pattern. Its foliage-shaped base makes it an elegant and unusual mug rest.

The design is made from a base panel of dark hardwood and a floral overlay in a lighter shade of hardwood. The finish is a coat of heatproof varnish or lacquer. Optionally, you can apply a thin sheet of cork to the underside of the base panel for added protection to vulnerable polished surfaces.

If you wish to make up a batch of these mug rests, there is no reason why several cannot be made in a 'sandwich' to save cutting time (see 'Stack sawing', page 8). Using 3–4mm (⅛in) hardwood means that you can batch several together to cut out simultaneously; this is not beyond the capacity of even the smallest of scrollsaws. To begin cutting, either singly or stacked, make up the bases first and use a second cutting pattern to lay out the parts. This is especially

The completed mug rests in use

Cutting the floral parts from a sheet of 3mm (⅛in) walnut

important for the flower overlay as many of the parts are so similar; otherwise, you might find identifying and gluing down the separate pieces problematic. Cut out all the parts and shape them with the drum sander in the minidrill. When all the parts have been cut and shaped, use the minimum of glue to secure them to their bases; this is to avoid seepage.

In terms of decoration, using two attractive, contrasting hardwoods may be enough. Therefore, to finish, simply apply a coat of protective lacquer to render them impervious to heat from a mug of tea or coffee.

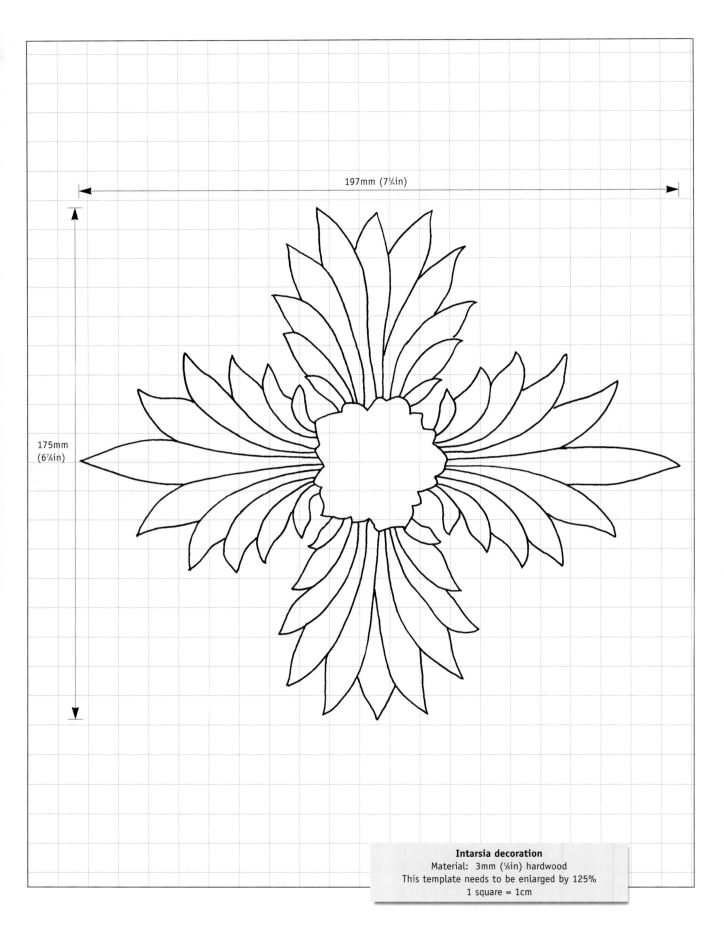

197mm (7¾in)

175mm (6⅞in)

Intarsia decoration
Material: 3mm (⅛in) hardwood
This template needs to be enlarged by 125%
1 square = 1cm

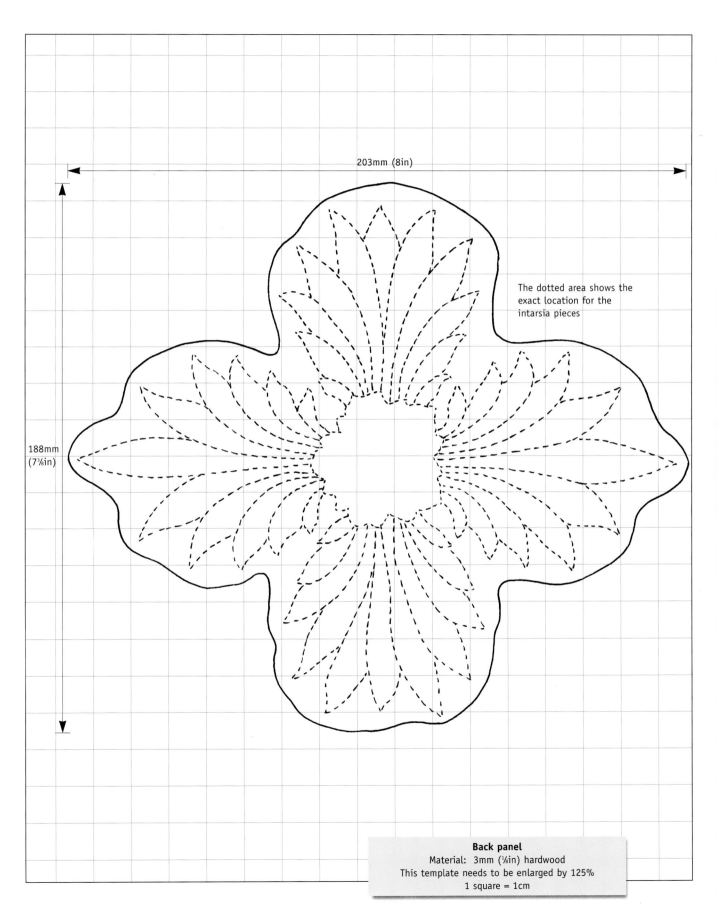

203mm (8in)

188mm
(7⅜in)

The dotted area shows the
exact location for the
intarsia pieces

Back panel
Material: 3mm (⅛in) hardwood
This template needs to be enlarged by 125%
1 square = 1cm

Swans ring tray

This project is great for exploiting intarsia's potential for three-dimensional designs. The ring tray is composed of a decorative background panel depicting a swan and cygnets and a two-part base which can be used to hold small items of jewellery. For simplicity, I have painted the swans on the panel and varnished the wood base.

Begin your design by making up a set of cutting patterns and sticking them down onto your wood. The base forms a sandwich of two pieces of wood; the upper part only includes the cutout to form the tray. Make up the sandwich for the base and, at this stage, cut around the exterior only. Once this external cut is complete (which ensures that both the top and bottom of the base match precisely), remove the bottom piece from the sandwich and make the internal cutout which forms the tray itself.

At this point, drill the clearance holes for the screws to attach the background panel to the base. Remember to countersink the holes from the underside of the top. By making the screw holes for securing the base in this way, once the base has been assembled, there will be no screw holes visible, even from the bottom.

Once you have cut out the two base parts and drilled the holes for the back panel, cut out the bottom section of the panel. Shape this in the normal fashion, then glue and screw firmly to the upper part of the base. Now glue the bottom of the base into position and clamp together while the glue dries.

While you wait, complete the cutting out of the swans on the panel. Shape all the parts as they are cut out, and decorate as desired.

Assemble the swans panel and, to finish, add rubber self-adhesive feet or a thin sheet of cork to the underside of the ring tray to protect polished surfaces.

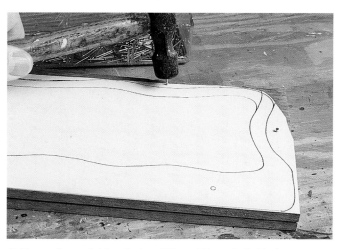

Making up the sandwich, prior to cutting out the parts for the base

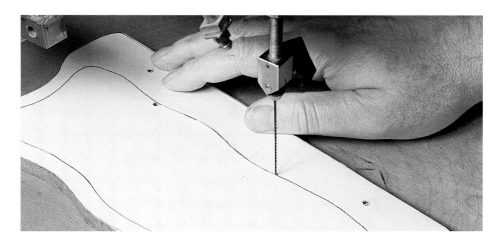

Making the internal cutout to form the tray on the upper section of the base

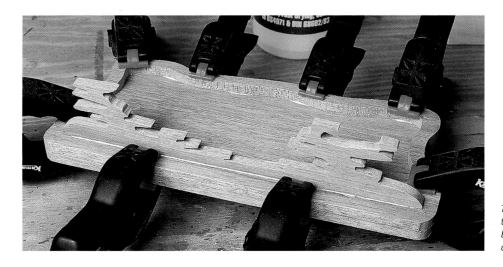

The assembled base with the lower part of the background panel, glued and clamped to dry

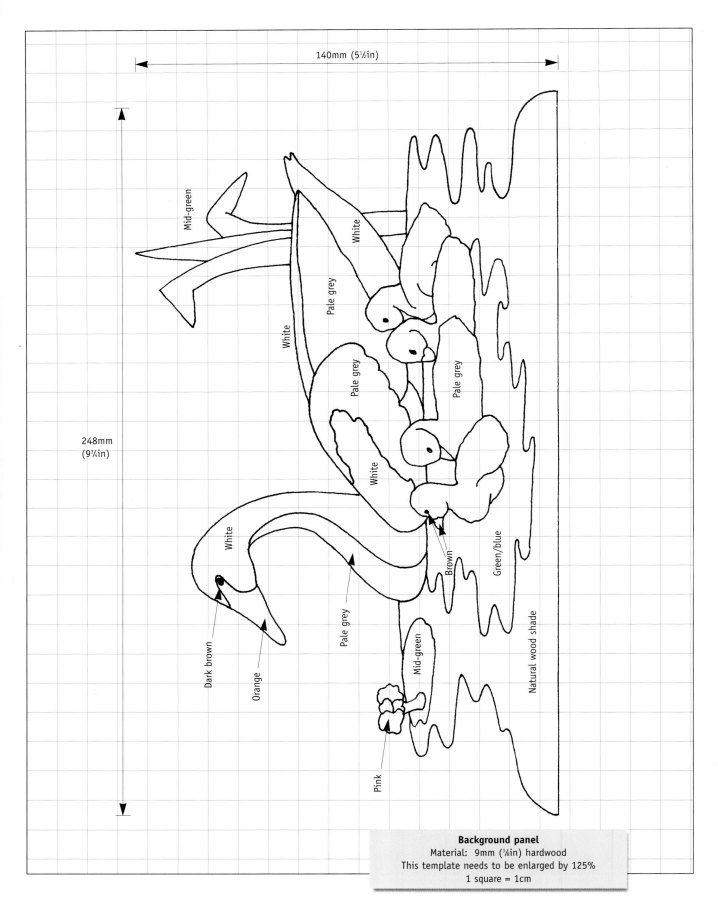

140mm (5½in)

248mm (9¾in)

Mid-green

White

Pale grey

White

Pale grey

Pale grey

White

White

Dark brown

Orange

Pale grey

Brown

Green/blue

Natural wood shade

Mid-green

Pink

Background panel
Material: 9mm (⅜in) hardwood
This template needs to be enlarged by 125%
1 square = 1cm

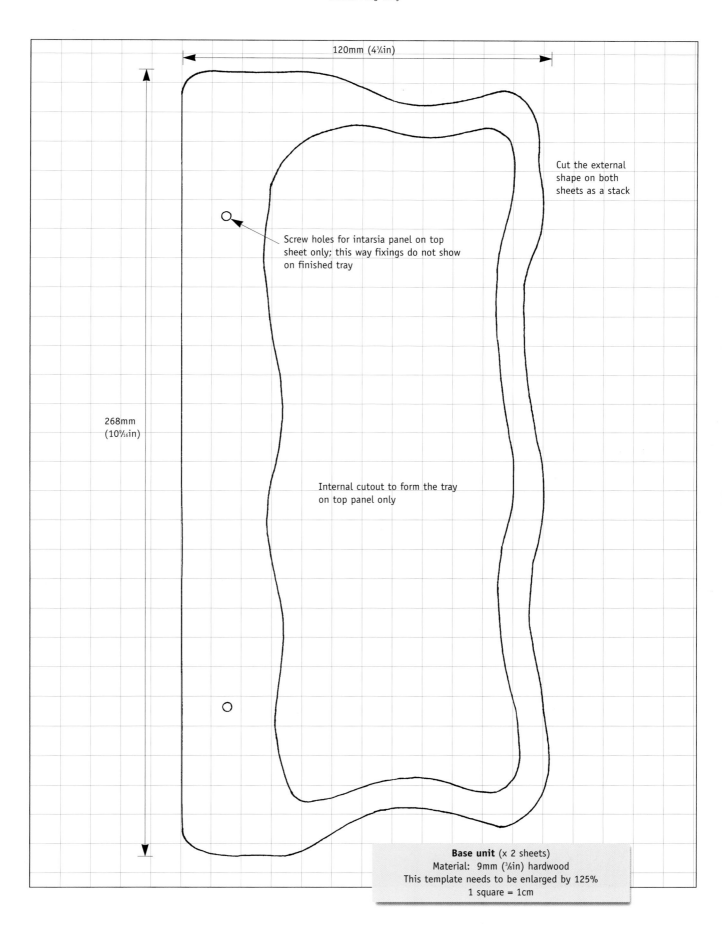

120mm (4¾in)

268mm
(10⁹⁄₁₆in)

Cut the external
shape on both
sheets as a stack

Screw holes for intarsia panel on top
sheet only; this way fixings do not show
on finished tray

Internal cutout to form the tray
on top panel only

Base unit (x 2 sheets)
Material: 9mm (³⁄₈in) hardwood
This template needs to be enlarged by 125%
1 square = 1cm

Coat rack

This brightly coloured rack, featuring intarsia butterflies and leaves, is great for hanging coats and hats, and is easily adaptable to other uses, too. Its bold appeal may even persuade small children to tidy their clothes!

The backing plate, which fastens the finished item to a door or wall, can be secured with a couple of keyhole plates so that it will sit flush. If you look at the template, you will note that you need to pre-drill clearance holes for the hooks to pass through the leaf and butterfly motifs into the back piece, which carries the weight. The design shows five hooks but you can, of course, alter this number to fit your own requirements.

Once you have cut and shaped the parts for the front panel, decorate as you like.

Now assemble the coat rack, beginning with the butterflies as these are not fully supported by the back panel. Allow the glue on these parts to dry completely before completing the piece. Finish with a coat of protective varnish so that fingermarks can easily be wiped away.

Finally, attach mirror plates to the back of the rack for mounting on the wall.

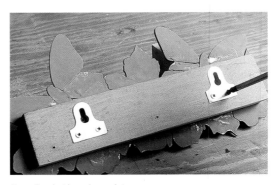

Screwing in the mirror plates

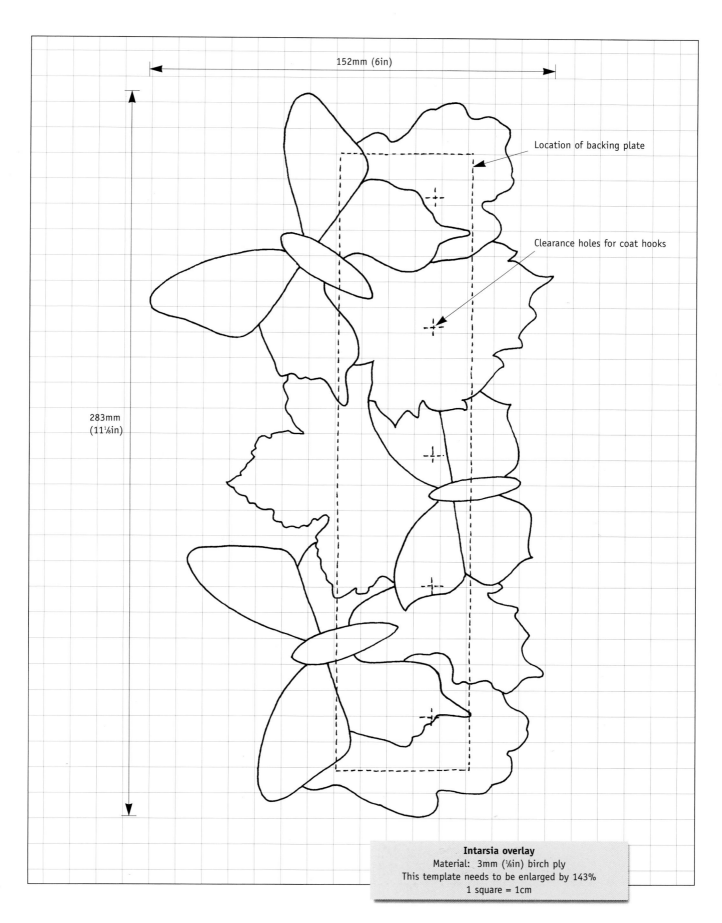

152mm (6in)

283mm
(11⅛in)

Location of backing plate

Clearance holes for coat hooks

Intarsia overlay
Material: 3mm (⅛in) birch ply
This template needs to be enlarged by 143%
1 square = 1cm

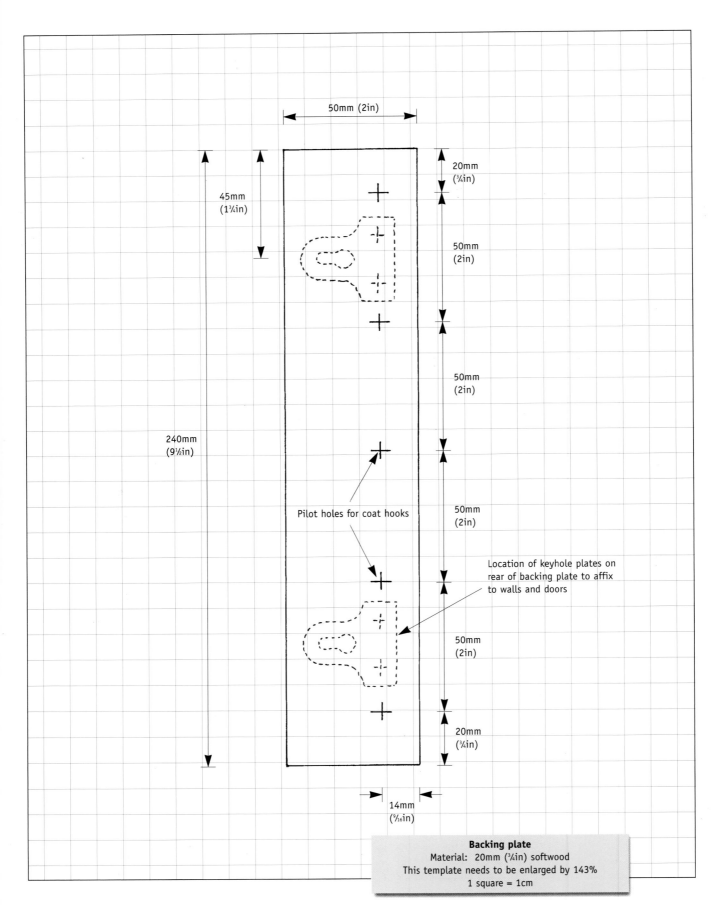

50mm (2in)

45mm
(1¾in)

240mm
(9½in)

20mm
(¾in)

50mm
(2in)

50mm
(2in)

50mm
(2in)

50mm
(2in)

20mm
(¾in)

14mm
(⁹⁄₁₆in)

Pilot holes for coat hooks

Location of keyhole plates on
rear of backing plate to affix
to walls and doors

Backing plate
Material: 20mm (¾in) softwood
This template needs to be enlarged by 143%
1 square = 1cm

Plate stand

This plate stand is very different from the norm and would look great in a high-tech kitchen or dining room, decorated to match your decor. The design can be duplicated as many times as you like for a complete set. The material is only 6mm (¼in) thick, enabling you to stack several layers of blanks into a sandwich to reduce cutting time.

The pieces that make up the plate stand are quite large and should pose little problem, but take care to cut the pieces accurately; the straight lines and circular sections will otherwise look distinctly odd.

To protect vulnerable polished surfaces when the plate stands are in use, I recommend adding a thin layer of cork to their underside. When cutting your circular

cutout, just ensure that it fits neatly between the bars of the T-shaped pieces so that it is invisible on the display side of the stand.

Gluing a protective cork base to the plate stand

240mm (9½in)

Abstract plate stand
Material: 6–9mm (¼–⅜in) ply
This template needs to be enlarged by 143%
1 square = 1cm

Celtic mirror frame

This striking design uses intarsia to enhance the scallop-shaped ends of an otherwise plain, dark-varnished wooden mirror frame. To make the piece lightweight, the basic frame has been made from a sheet of 6mm (¼in) hardwood.

Many designs for mirror and picture frames in scrollwork tend to be a little chunky and I have consciously avoided this in my design. The decorative overlay is inspired by a Celtic knotwork pattern, and was made from a thickish piece of brass sheeting.

Naturally, cutting thick brass and shaping it in intarsia takes rather a long time and calls not only for metal-cutting blades, but a lot of care handling them. If you want to, substitute the brass overlay with a light shade of wood and it will look equally attractive, but I thought it useful to demonstrate the potential for mixing materials in your designs.

Similarly, while this design is for a mirror frame, there is no reason why you could not substitute the mirror for a piece of picture glass to show off a photograph; you may simply need to add a sheet of card between them. Alternatively, you can make the frame and backing piece that securely retains the mirror or picture in place of a thinner material so that both picture glass and photograph fully occupy the space.

Making up the sandwich of front and mirror-retaining panels

Drilling the starter holes for the internal cutouts on the front panel

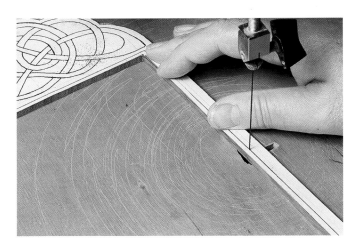

The frame of the mirror comes in two parts. To retain a mirror you need an aperture in the frame which is smaller than the backing for the frame in order to hold it in place. To effect this, you need two pieces of wood to make up a sandwich for the front panel and retaining frame and backing for the frame. The front part should be hardwood but you can use 3mm (⅛in) ply or MDF for the backing panel. The backing need be only a little larger than the mirror cutout and can also be made of 3mm (⅛in) ply or MDF. Having made up the sandwich for the front panel and the retaining frame with the wood front panel on top, pin the two pieces together and stick down your cutting pattern.

Begin by making the external cutout on both pieces of the sandwich. This ensures that the outlines of both pieces are identical. The internal cutouts will differ in size from the external, requiring a smaller cutout in the front panel than the back to support the mirror and prevent it from falling out of its frame. The cutting pattern for the front panel is the correct size for the mirror cutout so that this doesn't happen. The separate pattern for the mirror-retaining panel gives the dimensions for the cutout for the retaining panel. If you are using a mirror that varies from the dimensions given then you will need to adapt these to suit your own mirror. Whatever you use, allow approximately 4mm (⅛in) overlap to ensure the mirror or picture glass is adequately retained.

Once you have cut out the front panel and mirror-retaining panel, turn to the decorative overlay and the panel securing the

Completing the internal cutout on the front panel

Checking the mirror size before removing the cutting pattern from the front panel

mirror. The latter is simply a rectangle of the appropriate size to cover the retaining panel and to secure the mirror in place. You will need a spare cutting pattern for the decorative overlay as several of the pieces are similar in size and shape and using one will prevent any confusion as you figure out what cutout goes where.

With your cutout parts, begin to assemble the mirror frame. Glue the decorative overlay pieces onto the front panel and allow the glue to dry thoroughly. Attach the mirror-retaining frame with glue, clamp and allow to dry. Now insert the mirror. Do not glue this into position – the wood of the frame may move in response to changes in temperature and humidity and the mirror will crack if already secured. Once the mirror is in place, screw down the back retaining panel and, to finish, apply a couple of coats of varnish.

Laying out the cutting patterns for the decorative overlay onto thick brass sheet

Using the minidrill to shape the brass pieces before positioning them on the front panel

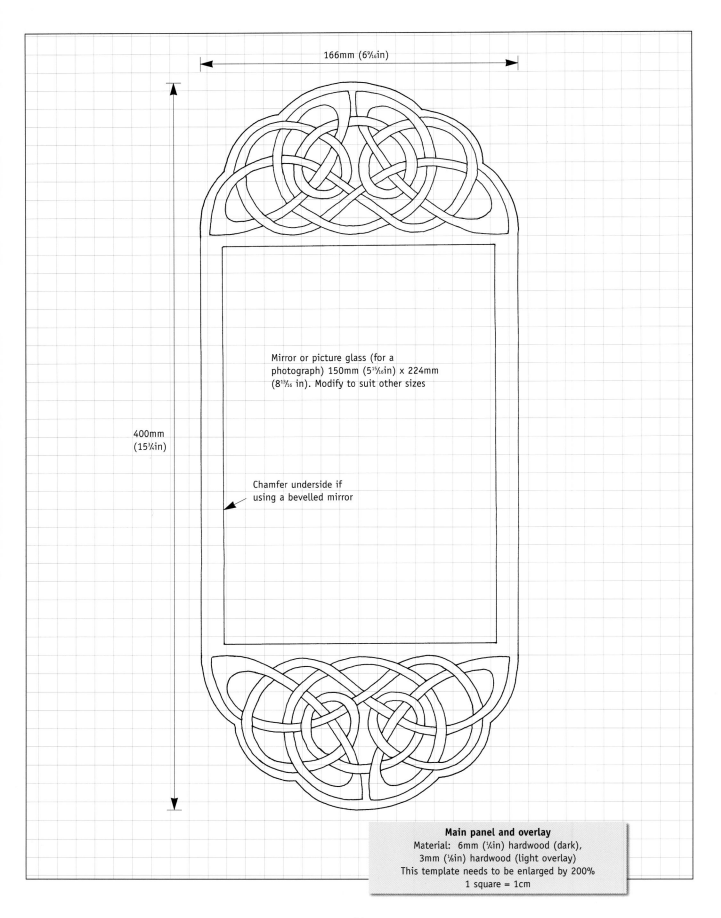

166mm (6⁹⁄₁₆in)

400mm (15¾in)

Mirror or picture glass (for a photograph) 150mm (5¹⁵⁄₁₆in) x 224mm (8¹³⁄₁₆ in). Modify to suit other sizes

Chamfer underside if using a bevelled mirror

Main panel and overlay
Material: 6mm (¼in) hardwood (dark),
3mm (⅛in) hardwood (light overlay)
This template needs to be enlarged by 200%
1 square = 1cm

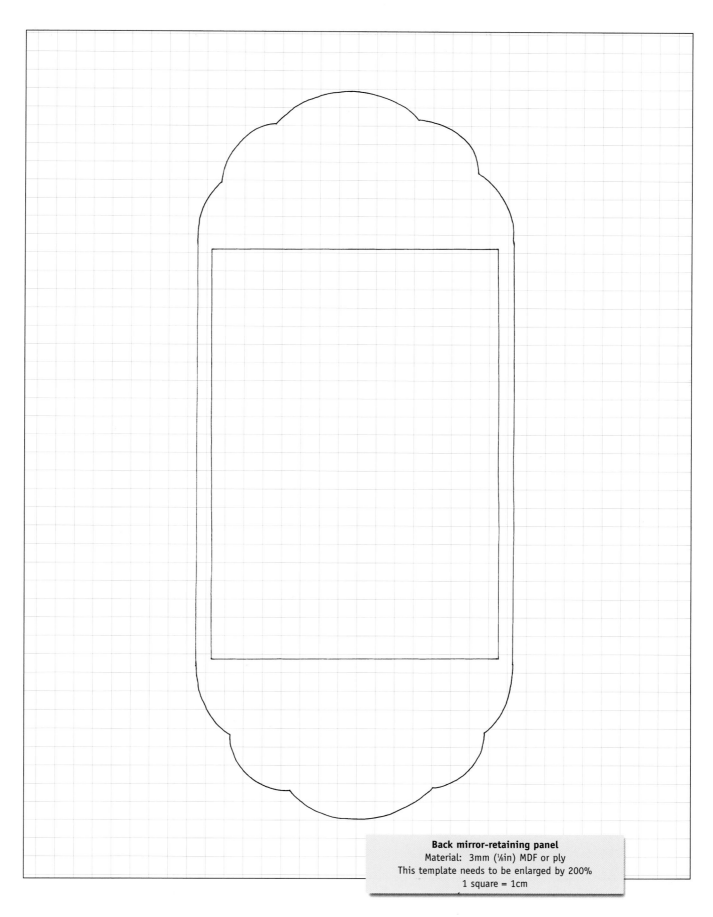

Back mirror-retaining panel
Material: 3mm (⅛in) MDF or ply
This template needs to be enlarged by 200%
1 square = 1cm

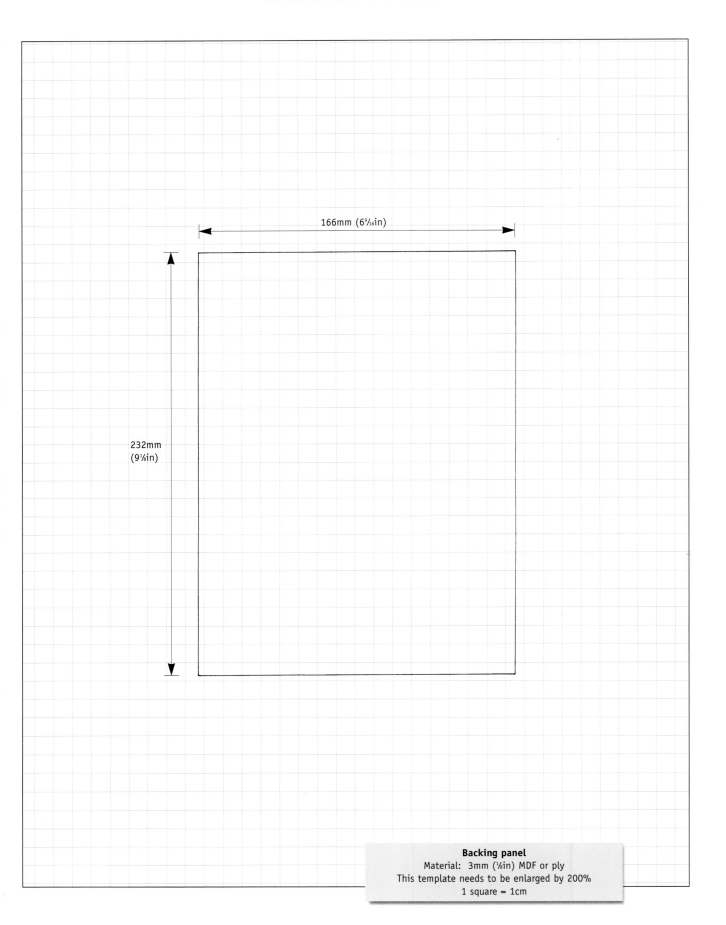

166mm (6⁹⁄₁₆in)

232mm
(9¹⁄₈in)

Backing panel
Material: 3mm (⅛in) MDF or ply
This template needs to be enlarged by 200%
1 square = 1cm

Woodsman's box

This attractive box will prove eminently suitable for the storage of personal effects, making use of intarsia patterns as decorative overlay on all four sides and the lid. The front and one further side show a woodland scene pattern, mirrored on the back and remaining side. The lid is bevel cut to produce a three-tiered effect and then decorated with oak leaf and acorn motifs. The whole thing is finished off with decorative brass feet and an antique style brass knob for the lid.

The description may sound complex and difficult to make but it really isn't daunting. With a little care and attention to detail, it is well within the capabilities of most scrollsaw users. In addition to your scrollsaw and minidrill, a set of corner clamps are particularly useful if you have them. Using corner clamps ensures you set the sides of the box perfectly square and everything else will then fall into place.

Begin by cutting out the top, bottom and sides so that you start with a set of pre-cut panels. See the templates for the required sizes. Once you have the basic box components ready cut, check your cutting pattern for size against the side panels you already have. The overlay should fit the side panels exactly. At this point you can adjust the size of your cutting pattern at your local photocopy shop to accurately fit the side panels and prevent gaps.

Once you are happy with the overlay patterns, assemble the four side panels as shown in the pattern and glue, pin and set them into the corner clamps to dry. Check once more that the size of your cutting patterns for the overlays are correct and then cut out the patterns. Round over the parts of your overlays and decorate to your preference or follow the colours shown on the original. Now stick the overlays into position on the side panels.

Check the position of the box section on your base panel, glue, then screw into place. If you are using brass feet, now is the time to fit them. If you don't have brass feet, others will do just as well – or you could add a thin sheet of cork to protect delicate surfaces.

All that remains to make is the box lid. You will need to drill small starter holes at an angle of approximately 5° as shown in the pattern for the bevel cuts. This will give the lid a three-tiered decorative effect. You can, of course, leave the lid flat for an alternative effect. Finish off by attaching a brass or wooden knob to the centre of the box lid.

Setting the box frame with a set of corner clamps for accurate right angles

Mounting the decorative intarsia pieces onto the side panels of the box

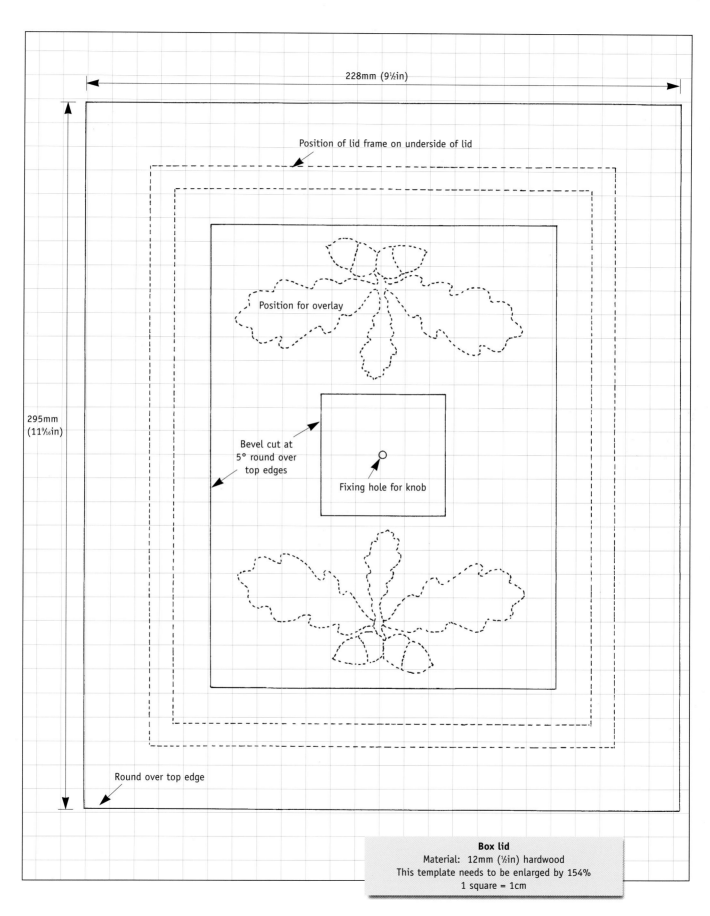

228mm (9½in)

Position of lid frame on underside of lid

Position for overlay

295mm
(11⅗in)

Bevel cut at
5° round over
top edges

Fixing hole for knob

Round over top edge

Box lid
Material: 12mm (½in) hardwood
This template needs to be enlarged by 154%
1 square = 1cm

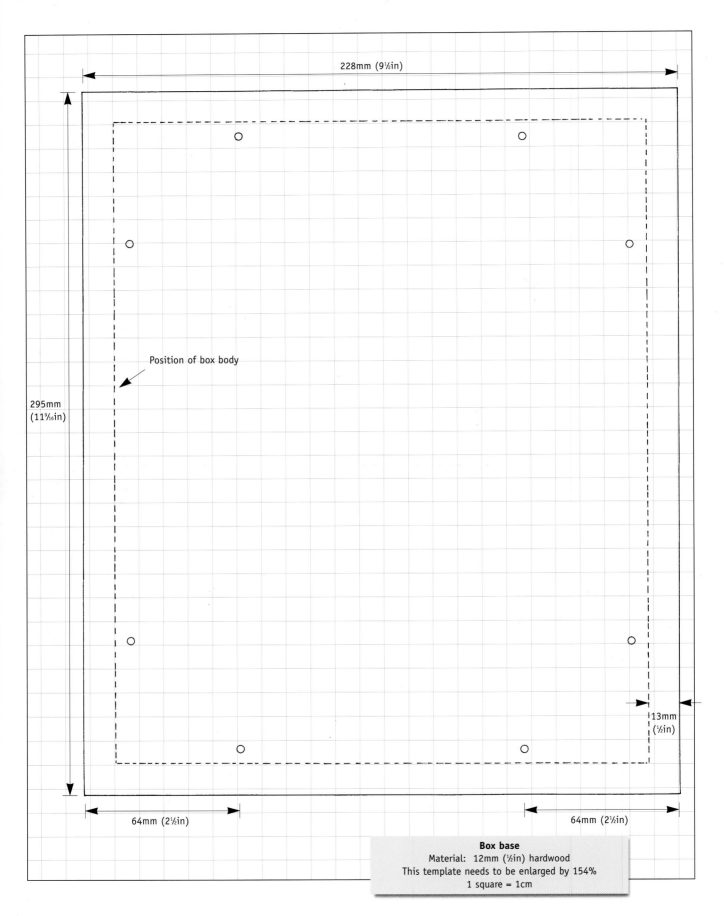

228mm (9½in)

295mm (11⁹⁄₁₆in)

Position of box body

13mm (½in)

64mm (2½in)

64mm (2½in)

Box base
Material: 12mm (½in) hardwood
This template needs to be enlarged by 154%
1 square = 1cm

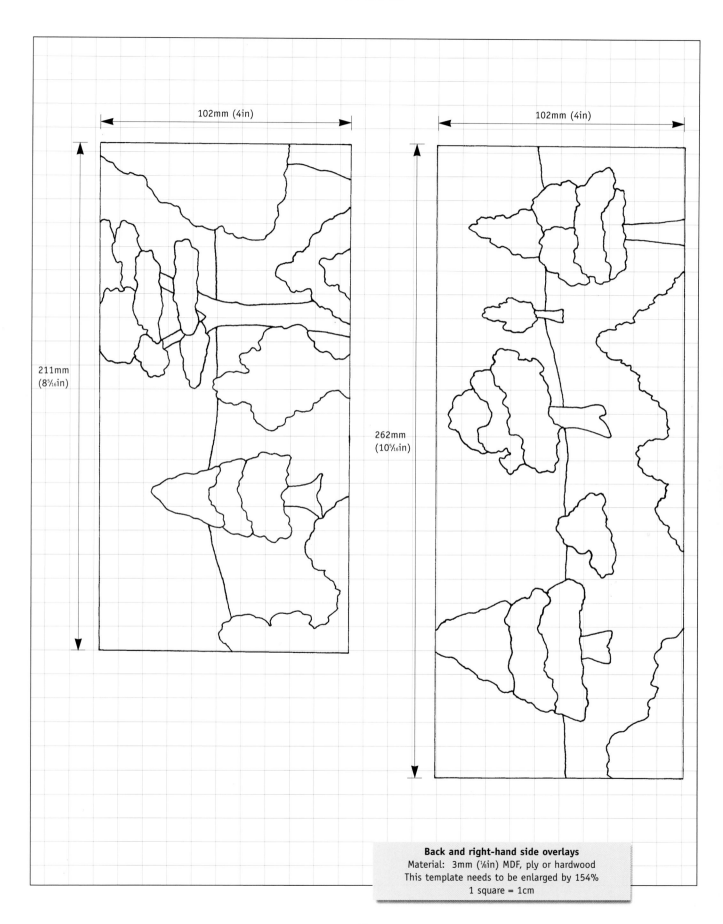

102mm (4in)

102mm (4in)

211mm
(8⁵⁄₁₆in)

262mm
(10⁵⁄₁₆in)

Back and right-hand side overlays
Material: 3mm (⅛in) MDF, ply or hardwood
This template needs to be enlarged by 154%
1 square = 1cm

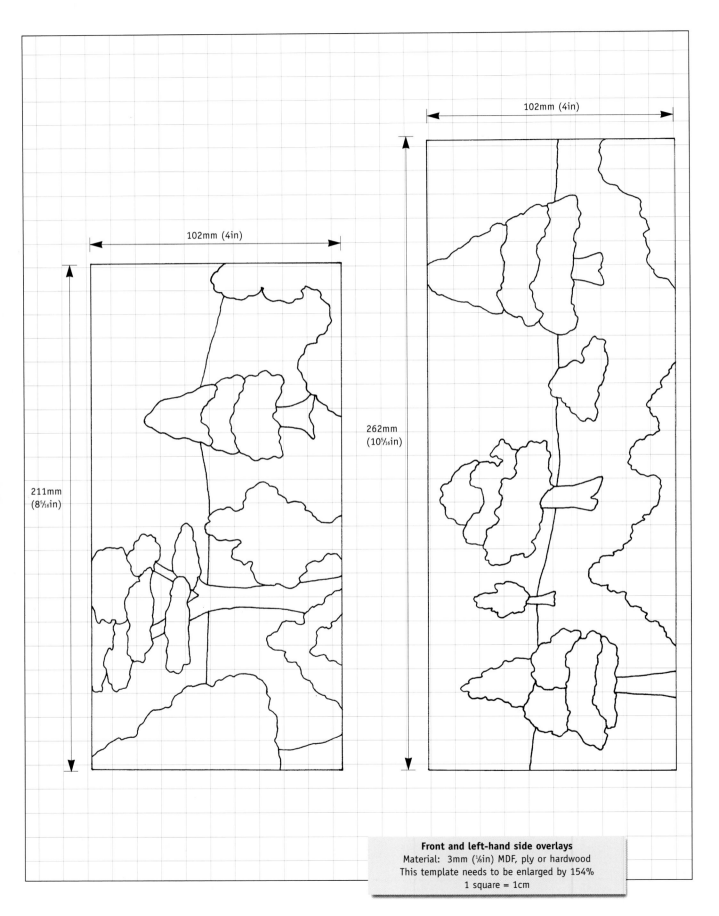

102mm (4in)

102mm (4in)

262mm
(10⁵⁄₁₆in)

211mm
(8⁵⁄₁₆in)

Front and left-hand side overlays
Material: 3mm (⅛in) MDF, ply or hardwood
This template needs to be enlarged by 154%
1 square = 1cm

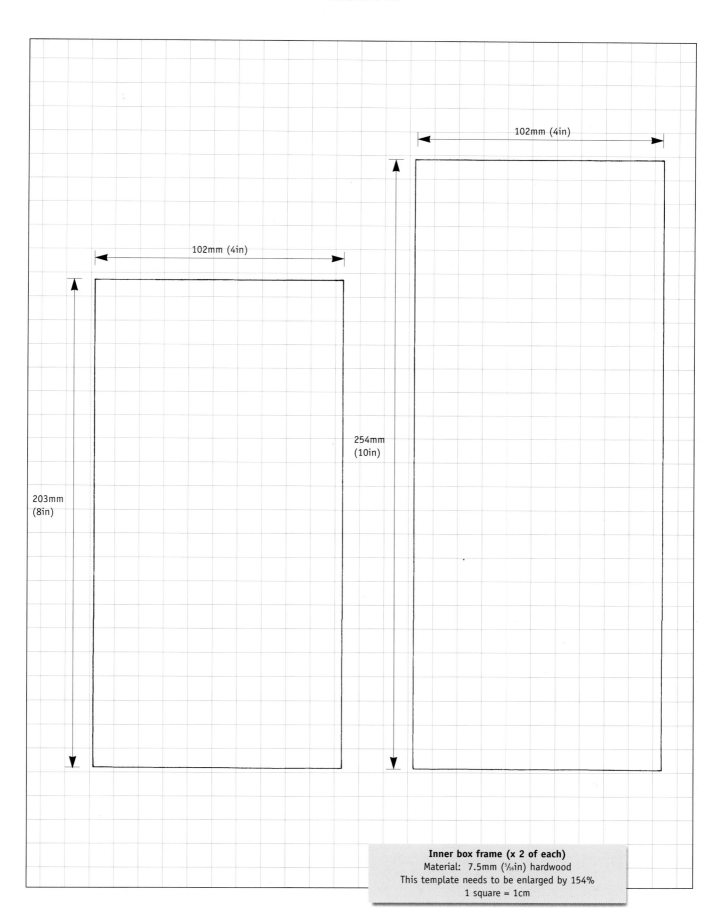

102mm (4in)

254mm
(10in)

102mm (4in)

203mm
(8in)

Inner box frame (x 2 of each)
Material: 7.5mm (⁵⁄₁₆in) hardwood
This template needs to be enlarged by 154%
1 square = 1cm

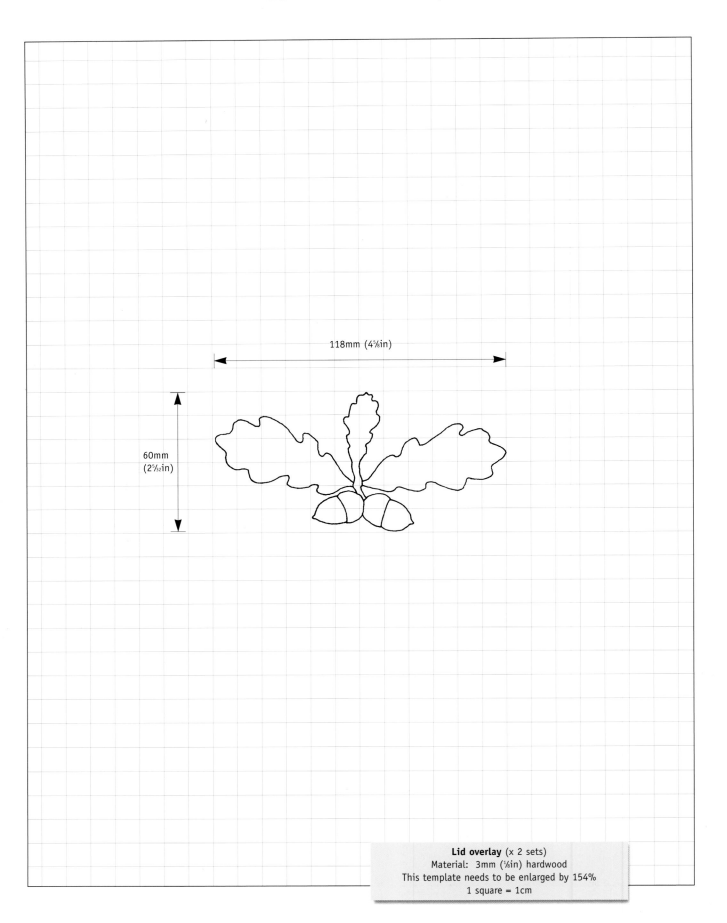

118mm (4⅝in)

60mm
(2⁵⁄₃₂in)

Lid overlay (x 2 sets)
Material: 3mm (⅛in) hardwood
This template needs to be enlarged by 154%
1 square = 1cm

Noughts and crosses board and pieces

This intarsia games board and pieces set will provide lots of fun for youngsters with its bright colours and bold design, all of which are cut on the scrollsaw, and should pose few problems even for a beginner. On the original shown here, I confess to cheating a little by using a Forstner bit in a pillar drill to cut away the centre of the noughts pieces but a starter hole and a scrollsaw blade will do the job just as well; it just takes a little longer to do. The board itself has 'pathways' left in the main area of wood to delineate the possible winning lines. These are coloured in the same way as the squares themselves to accentuate the possibilities.

If you have a pillar drill, make the cutouts in the centres of the noughts first or, alternatively, do it on your scrollsaw. Next cut

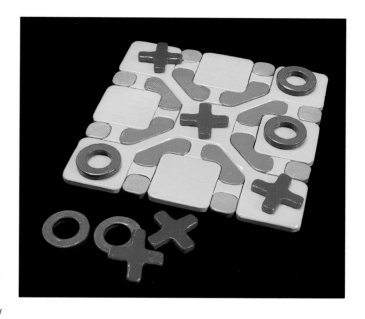

and shape the individual parts until you have the full set of pieces, and decorate them in brightly coloured child-safe paints such as acrylics or enamels.

Finally, glue the parts of the board together and apply a couple of coats of protective varnish so that the colours of the board remain vibrant for years to come.

Using a Forstner drill bit in a pillar drill to make the centres of the noughts

Cutting out the pieces on the scrollsaw

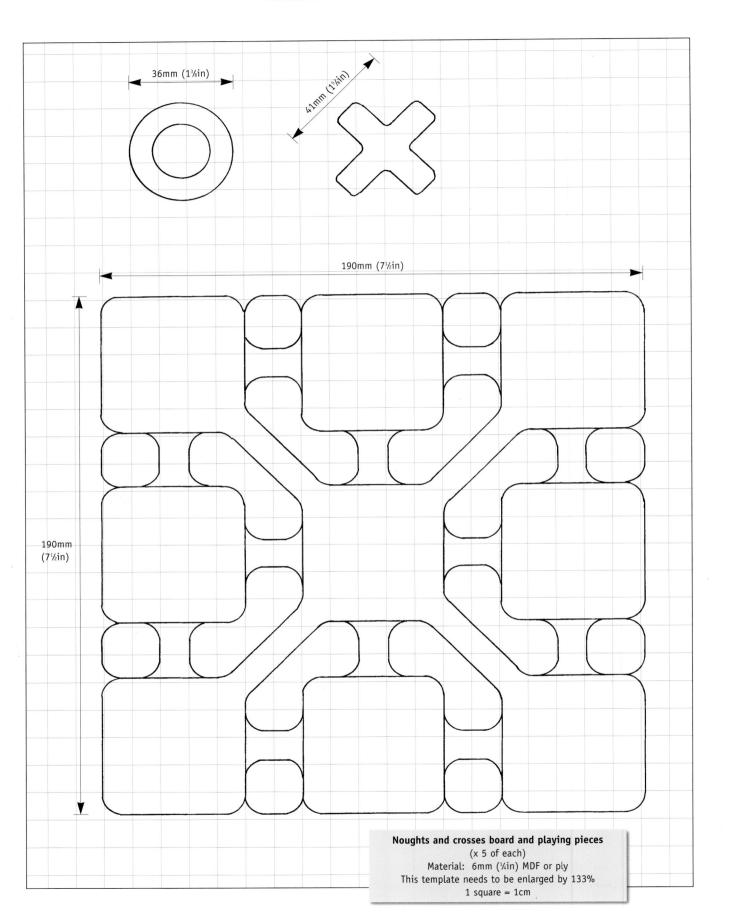

36mm (1⅜in)

41mm (1⅝in)

190mm (7½in)

190mm
(7½in)

Noughts and crosses board and playing pieces
(x 5 of each)
Material: 6mm (¼in) MDF or ply
This template needs to be enlarged by 133%
1 square = 1cm

Mosaic
chessboard

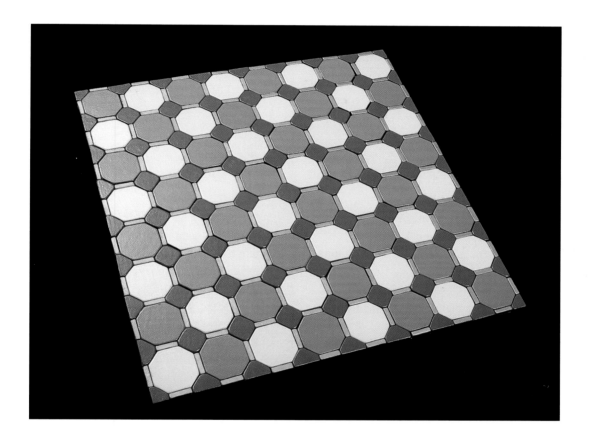

This project was originally intended as a decorative mosaic panel, but it occurred to me that perhaps it might have an interactive function, too. Don't be put off by the size of the finished chessboard, some 454mm (18¼in) square, especially if your scrollsaw only has a 400mm (16in) throat capacity. I have allowed for that by designing a template for a quarter of the design which can be repeated a further three times. All the parts are identical, thus enabling you to cut out a bit at a time and, providing you are reasonably accurate in

following the cutting lines, you will find that the same piece will fit anywhere within the design layout.

A spare copy of the cutting pattern will be helpful if you make it up into the full chessboard layout as shown in the templates. In this way you can place each part in its final position as you cut the pieces from the sheets and see immediately when you have sufficient pieces to complete the design. Once all the parts have been cut out, take another sheet of ply or MDF or whatever material you choose as

The cutting pattern is set firmly in place using Spray Mount

To ensure that you have the right quantity of pieces, cut out the individual parts and place onto the backing board as you work

a backing sheet for the board, and cut it to size. Now begin to round off all the parts of the design and place them into position onto the backing board as you work. Once you have shaped all the parts, close up any gaps between them so that you can judge if you need to make any small adjustments to the size of the backing board. There is often a small discrepancy even when using a very thin blade.

Trim the board to size. You are now ready to carry out the decoration of the mosaic pieces and glue them down onto the backing board.

I finished my chessboard in light and mid-grey enamel paint with intersecting sections of mid-blue and gold, and I think the result is very pleasing. For your own, however, you might like to experiment with a different colour combination.

Shaping the mosaic elements using a miniature drum sander fitted to the minidrill. The latter is mounted to a bench holder, leaving both hands free for shaping

Setting the decorated parts into place on the backing board

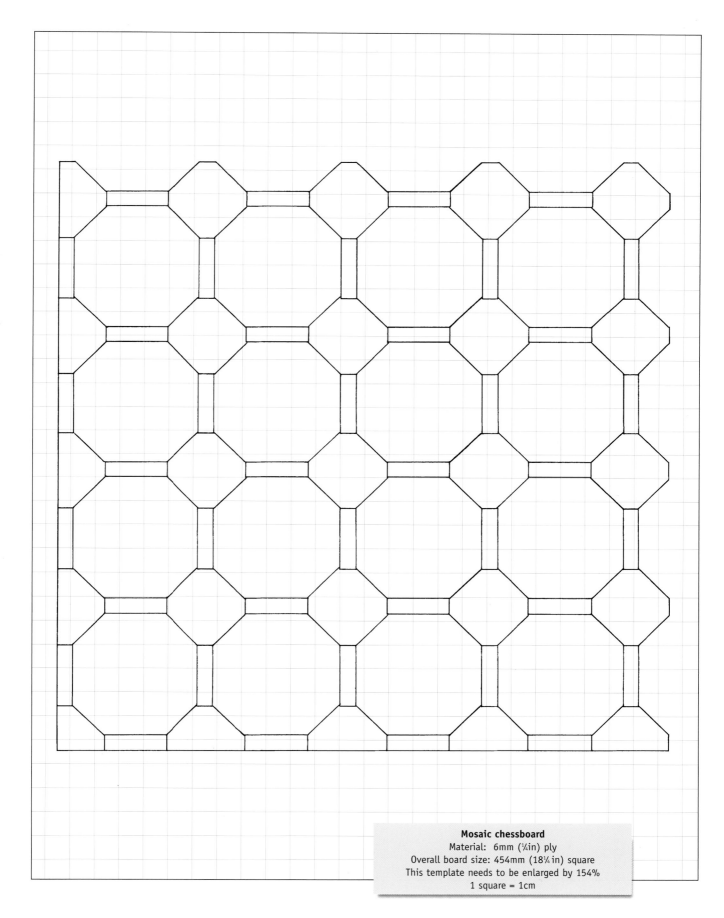

Mosaic chessboard
Material: 6mm (¼in) ply
Overall board size: 454mm (18¼in) square
This template needs to be enlarged by 154%
1 square = 1cm

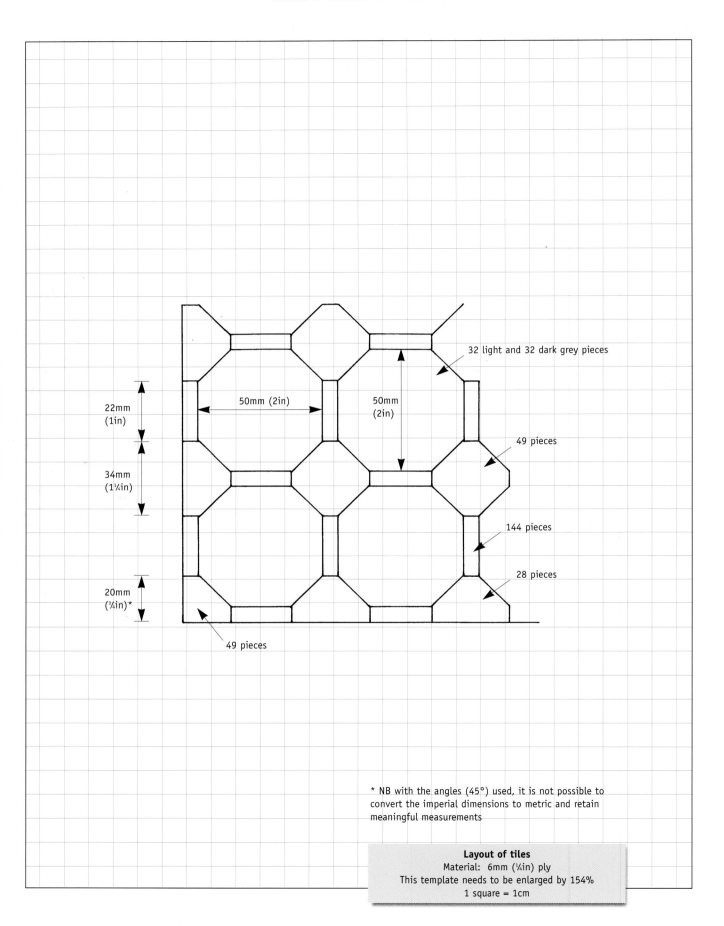

22mm
(1in)

50mm (2in)

50mm
(2in)

32 light and 32 dark grey pieces

34mm
(1¼in)

49 pieces

144 pieces

28 pieces

20mm
(¾in)*

49 pieces

* NB with the angles (45°) used, it is not possible to
convert the imperial dimensions to metric and retain
meaningful measurements

Layout of tiles
Material: 6mm (¼in) ply
This template needs to be enlarged by 154%
1 square = 1cm

Ribbons

This intarsia pattern was designed to make
use of offcuts and can be used to add
decorative relief to otherwise plain household
features such as doors and walls. The pattern
can be made either singly or, in the case of
the example shown here, in pairs, using a
sandwich of two different-coloured woods,
light cream obeche and dark brown iroko, to
form an attractive contrast. Many other
combinations would work equally well and you
can adapt to fit your own decor.

Once you have decided on the thickness
and colour of the woods you wish to use, it
is just a matter of cutting, shaping and then
arranging the pieces into a pattern, according
to preference. An additional copy of your
cutting pattern will be a distinct advantage
as an aid to identifying each piece as you
cut and shape it, but also so that you can
experiment with the arrangement of
contrasting colours.

After the cutting and shaping part of the
project is complete, take the pieces and apply
them to your chosen object or location. Once
mounted, apply a coat of varnish.

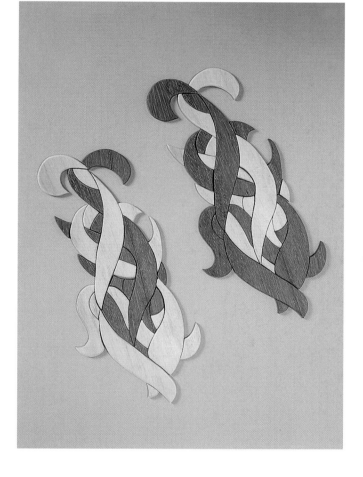

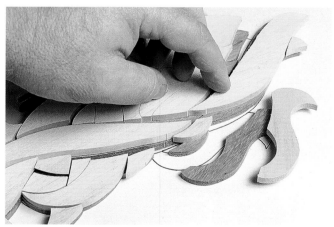

*Laying out the two sets of pieces on the spare pattern
before deciding on the final layout*

141mm (5½in)

313mm
(12⁵/₁₆in)

Make a sandwich of the two
contrasting woods and cut
them at the same time

Ribbons decoration
Material: 6mm (¼in) dark and light hardwoods
This template needs to be enlarged by 154%
1 square = 1cm

Dolphins

This pattern makes use of a popular dolphin motif which looks really effective fashioned in relief. The base panel of the piece forms the sea and is cut intarsia-style with spaces left for mounting the dolphins leaping across the waves.

You will need a few 20mm (¾in) brass or alternative panel pins together with a pilot hole, drill bit and cut-off disc for your minidrill to help you complete the project.

Begin with a set of cutting patterns in the usual way and stick these down onto your chosen base material with Spray Mount or other adhesive.

Sticking down the cutting patterns using Spray Mount adhesive

Cutting out the segments of the dolphin bodies on the scrollsaw

Cut out the base panel and the dolphin pieces and shape them using your minidrill fitted with a drum sander. Once cut and shaped, check that they fit well before decorating them and gluing them together. Make sure that the tenons on the bottoms of the dolphins form a tight fit into their respective slots on the base panel pieces.

Next decorate, then glue up first the bodies of the dolphins, and the base panel pieces together. Make a final check once your varnish or paint has dried, that the dolphins fit accurately into the base panel slots. Now drill pilot holes in the appropriate places in the dolphin bodies to fit the brass panel pins which form the bond for the fins. Use a pilot drill in your minidrill to prevent the wood splitting. Now gently tap in brass panel pins so that you have about 12mm (½in) left sticking out of the hole. Use your cut-off disc to remove the heads from the pins and drill corresponding pilot holes in the fins. Add a little epoxy resin adhesive to the join and tap home the fins, taking care not to bruise the wood. Touch up any decoration that may have been affected and complete the assembly.

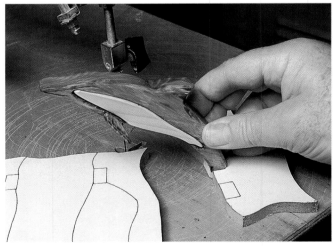

Tapping the brass panel pins into the pilot holes before fitting the fins

Mounting the dolphin to the base panel

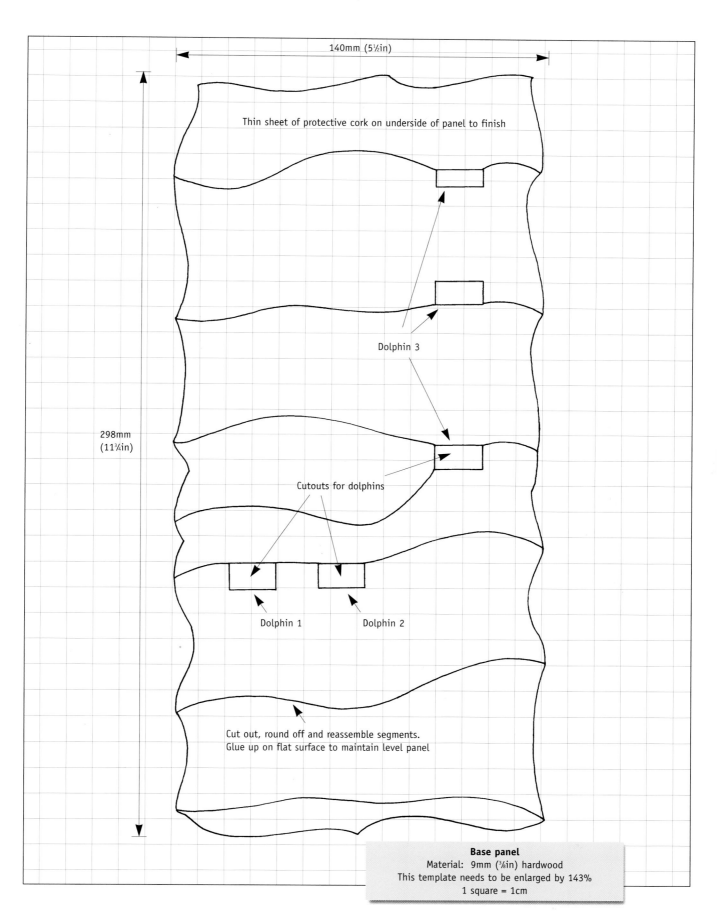

140mm (5½in)

298mm
(11¾in)

Thin sheet of protective cork on underside of panel to finish

Dolphin 3

Cutouts for dolphins

Dolphin 1   Dolphin 2

Cut out, round off and reassemble segments.
Glue up on flat surface to maintain level panel

Base panel
Material: 9mm (⅜in) hardwood
This template needs to be enlarged by 143%
1 square = 1cm

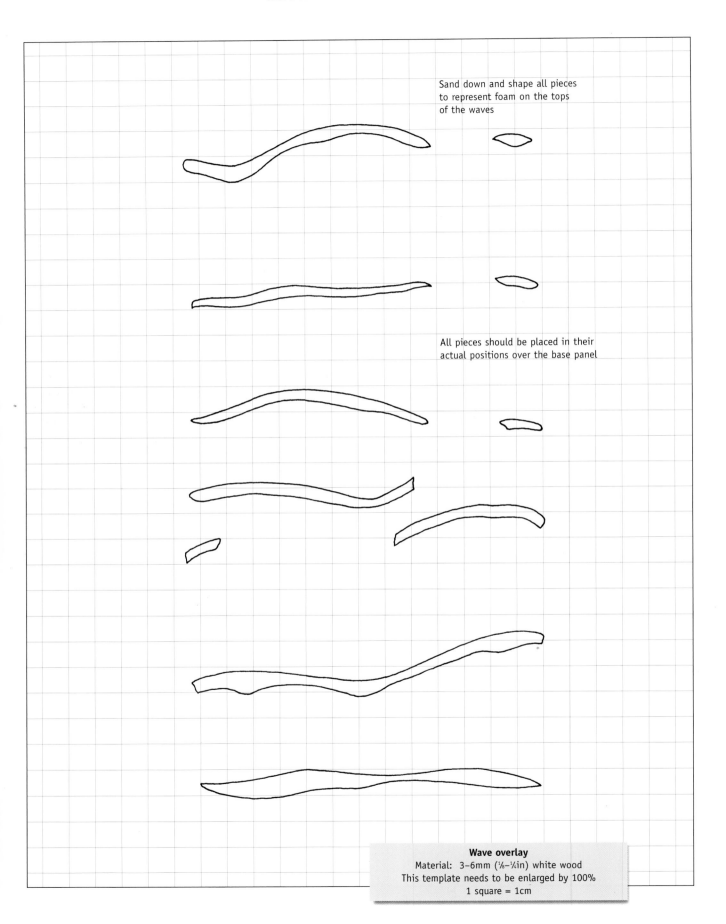

Sand down and shape all pieces
to represent foam on the tops
of the waves

All pieces should be placed in their
actual positions over the base panel

Wave overlay
Material: 3–6mm (⅛–¼in) white wood
This template needs to be enlarged by 100%
1 square = 1cm

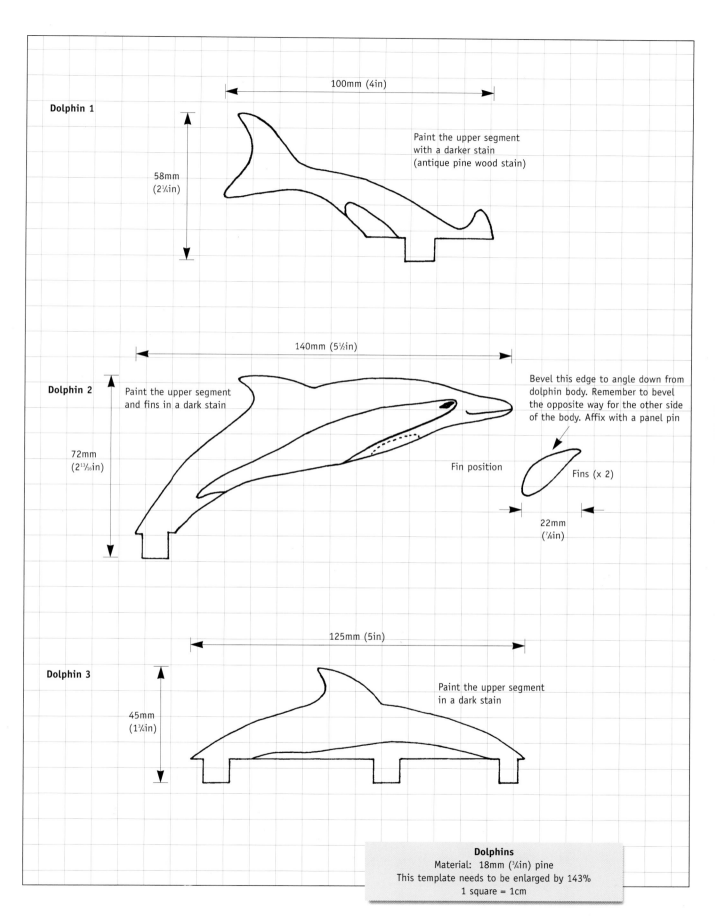

Dolphin 1

100mm (4in)

58mm
(2¼in)

Paint the upper segment
with a darker stain
(antique pine wood stain)

Dolphin 2

140mm (5½in)

Paint the upper segment
and fins in a dark stain

72mm
(2¹³⁄₁₆in)

Bevel this edge to angle down from
dolphin body. Remember to bevel
the opposite way for the other side
of the body. Affix with a panel pin

Fin position

Fins (x 2)

22mm
(⁷⁄₈in)

Dolphin 3

125mm (5in)

45mm
(1¾in)

Paint the upper segment
in a dark stain

Dolphins
Material: 18mm (¾in) pine
This template needs to be enlarged by 143%
1 square = 1cm

Cats

This model will be popular with all cat lovers. It is made from a piece of 20mm (¾in) hardwood to give the design sufficient width to be stable when freestanding. The wood used for the original, shown here, was recycled from an old and no longer required wardrobe and you might also like to make use of similar opportunities for a free supply of wood, while also being environmentally conscious.

Due to the freestanding nature of the project, you need to shape both front and back cutouts so that either side of the completed project looks good enough to display. The design incorporates some intricate pieces, so a false table for your scrollsaw will prove invaluable to prevent their loss.

Begin with a cutting pattern as usual, and make a spare copy of the pattern. This means you can lay out each part as it is cut and shaped and place it in its correct position straightaway. Cut out all the parts and then shape and decorate them in your own choice

Using a tapered burr in the minidrill to accentuate the saw kerf cuts which delineate the cat's claws

of cat-friendly colours. You can, if you prefer, simply rely on the character of the wood itself as a finish. When it comes to completing the cats' eyes, I have cut away the wood from this area and simply painted the inner surface of each in white; this is easier than carving them individually, as they are too tiny to handle.

Once you have cut, shaped and decorated all the pieces, begin gluing them together, leaving sufficient drying time between each batch, and ensuring that everything remains vertical as you work – or the finished model will not stand freely at all! Check how much glue you need; any excess has a tendency to seep from the sides and spoil the intarsia effect. Once finished, varnish with a protective coat or two to complete the piece.

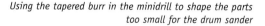

Using the tapered burr in the minidrill to shape the parts too small for the drum sander

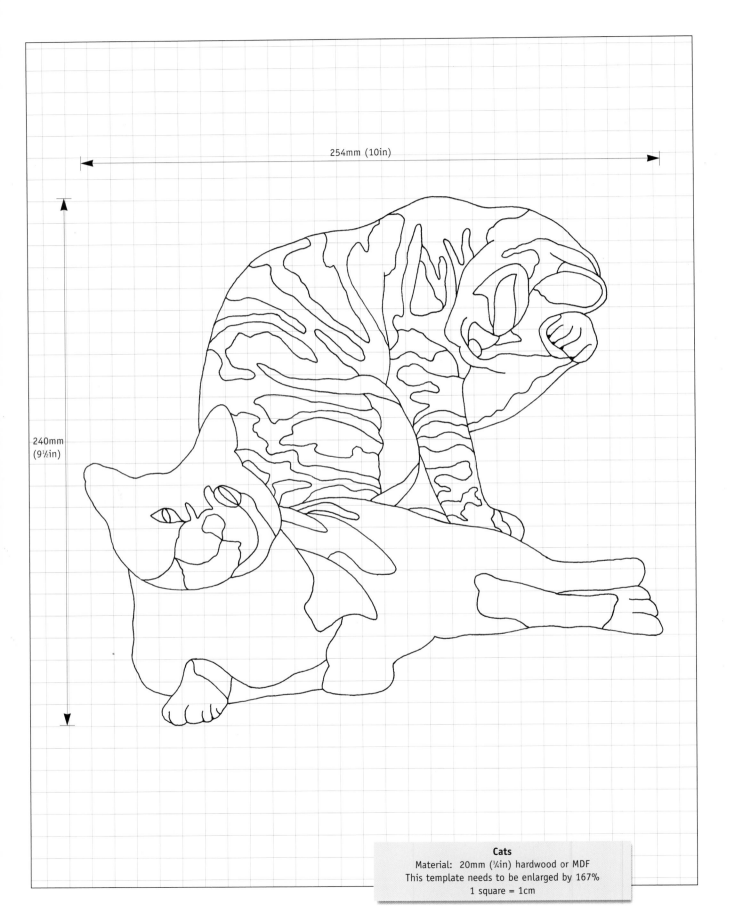

254mm (10in)

240mm
(9½in)

Cats
Material: 20mm (¾in) hardwood or MDF
This template needs to be enlarged by 167%
1 square = 1cm

1936 Mercedes coupé

This model of a classic Mercedes coupé has been made from a chunky piece of hardwood lending the piece a sense of depth – and also making it easy to handle and assemble. Some parts for the model require starter holes for the scrollsaw blade; using the minidrill with a very small drill bit is ideal for this task. Because the finished model is freestanding and can be viewed from each side, you will need to round over both aspects.

First, cut out your pattern, then cut out and clean up the plinth on which everything else will be mounted.

Next, cut out the section of wood which adjoins the plinth and on which the car's wheels will rest. Round this off on the top and sides – but not the bottom where the wood joins the plinth. Check carefully that this piece of wood sits at right angles to the base plinth before gluing firmly into place and, for

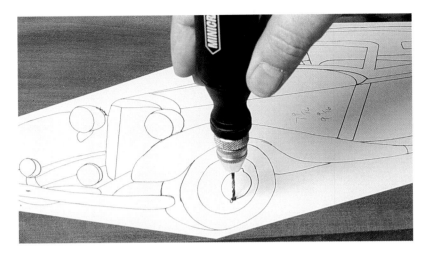

Using the minidrill to make starter holes in the wheels of the model car

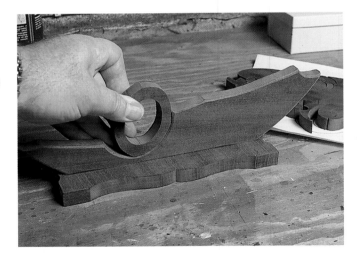

The base wood assembled on the plinth. The car's assembly begins with wheels and builds upwards from this point

added security, insert a couple of small screws from the underside of the piece, too.

Begin cutting out the parts of the car itself. It is easiest if you start with the wheels so that you can round off and glue each part into place onto the base as you go. Carry on until all the pieces have been cut out, shaped and fitted together. Take care as you glue each one into place, that it is even on both sides of the growing assembly and that everything remains at right angles.

The finished model shown here has been left unpainted, and given only a coat of satin varnish to accentuate the grain of the wood. You may prefer to paint your model in the colours of your own choosing rather than leave bare wood, particularly if you are using a cheaper wood such as pine.

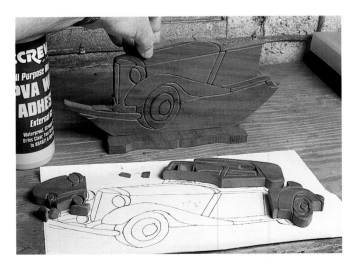

Assembly in progress

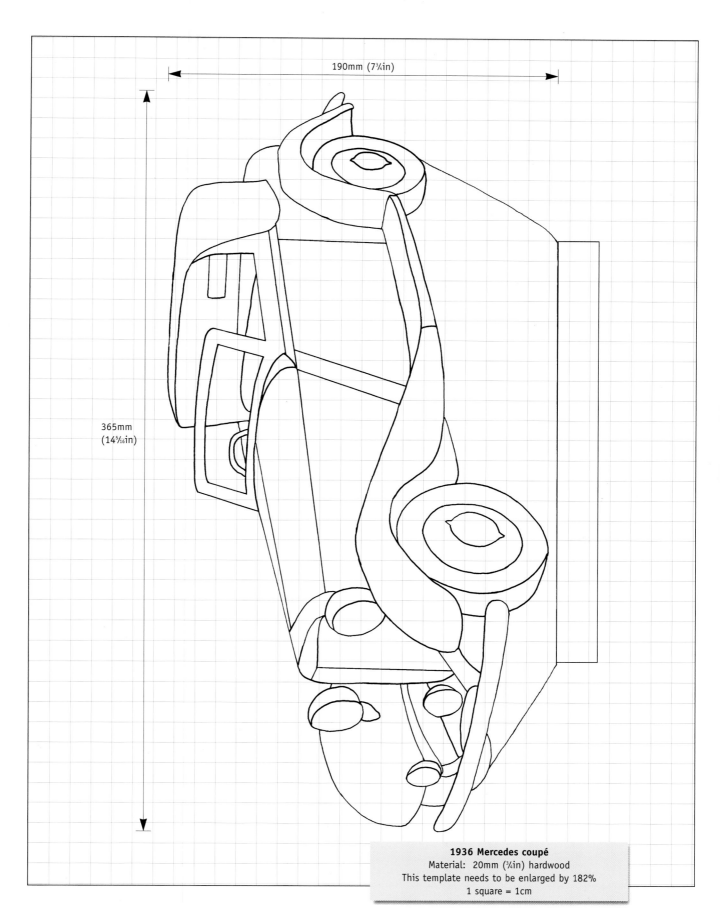

190mm (7¾in)

365mm
(14⁵⁄₁₆in)

1936 Mercedes coupé
Material: 20mm (¾in) hardwood
This template needs to be enlarged by 182%
1 square = 1cm

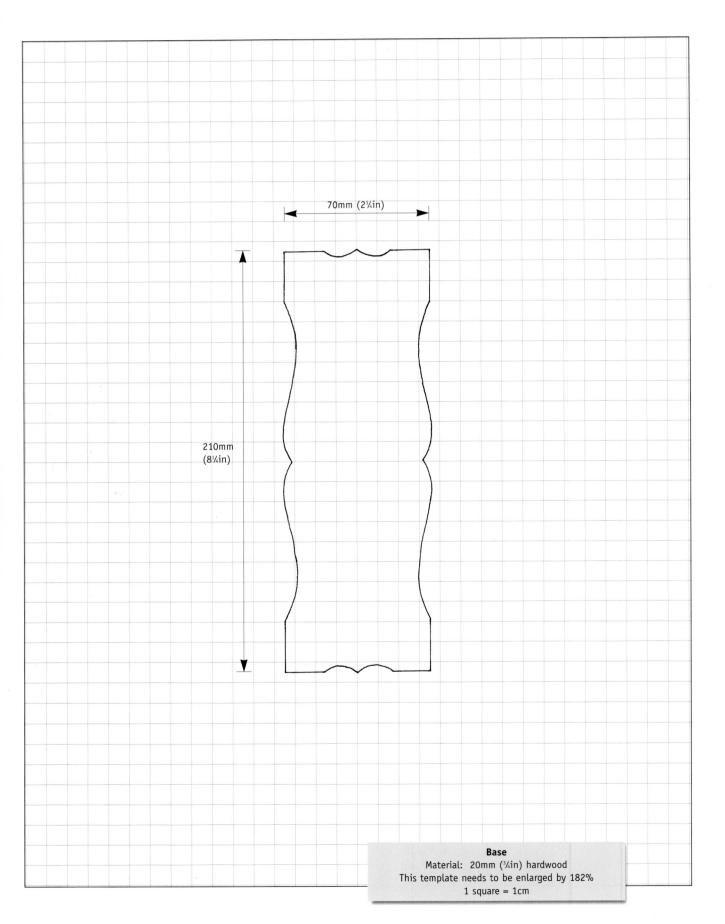

70mm (2¾in)

210mm
(8¼in)

Base
Material: 20mm (¾in) hardwood
This template needs to be enlarged by 182%
1 square = 1cm

Rose

This little panel is straightforward to make and is an attractive addition to any wall in your home. The original, shown here, was made from 9mm (⅜in) hardwood, finished in metallic varnish, bonded onto a dark-stained wood panel and then framed. The combination of the thickness of the wood for the rose and the intarsia treatment itself gives the finished flower an added depth.

Make up a cutting pattern to your required finished size and stick it into position on a hardwood panel. For the model shown here, I was able to obtain some wood from the frame of an old piano, supplied to me by a local dealer; perhaps you will also have a similar opportunity and, if you do, always take advantage of it. Because the background is to be stained dark and the actual rose finished in a bright-coloured varnish, the type of wood you use is relatively unimportant; pretty well anything you have close to hand will be adequate.

Cut out the segments of the flower and shape them using the drum sander attached to your minidrill. Round over the edges of each piece thoroughly to emphasize the three-dimensionality of the rose.

In order to centre the rose on the backing panel before gluing into place, it is handy to cut out a spare cutting pattern for the outer border of the rose to the size and shape of the backing panel so that you can then remove the flower design from the centre, leaving an accurate cutout, which enables you to lay out the pieces and glue them in exactly the right places on the backing sheet.

Once that part is complete, simply add a frame to the panel with hanging eyes and your project is finished.

Ensuring the rose design is centred on the backing panel

Dark orange

Green

Green

Green

Green

Green

Rose panel
Material: 9mm (⅜in) hardwood
This template needs to be enlarged by 100%
1 square = 1cm

Douglas DC-3 'Dakota'

The design for this intarsia wall plaque depicts possibly the best known aircraft from the 1930s still flying today. It is made in 12mm (½in) hardwood to give it sufficient rigidity to stand freely without the need for a backing panel. The original shown here was made in oak and only minor details picked out in silver and gunmetal paint to leave a solid wood finish. You can, if you prefer, paint the whole thing. The addition of a picture hanging attachment to the back of your completed model allows its distinctive shape to stand out against the background.

Make a spare copy of the cutting pattern to help you lay out the individual pieces as you cut them on your scrollsaw. Begin by cutting out the aircraft parts and shaping the cutout pieces on the drum sander on your minidrill. As you complete each piece, position it onto the spare cutting pattern to make the assembly a more straightforward process.

Once you have all the parts cut out and in position, decorate as you wish then glue them together, taking care not to use too much glue or it may seep out and stick the aircraft and the pattern together. Once the glue has dried thoroughly, sand off any sticky bits of pattern and apply a coat of varnish to protect the finish.

The last step is to add a picture hanger. In order to ensure that it hangs straight on the wall, place the completed aircraft over the length of a ruler. The point at which it balances on the ruler without tipping over is the centre – and where you should place the hanger. Screw it into the back of the aircraft.

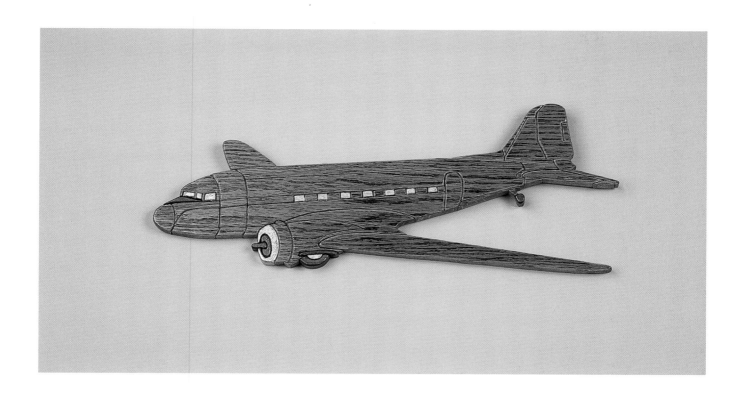

*Laying out the pieces on
the spare cutting pattern
as they are cut out on
the scrollsaw*

*The decorated pieces of
the aircraft ready for
final assembly*

*Locating the balancing
point of the completed
model to mount the
picture hanging attachment*

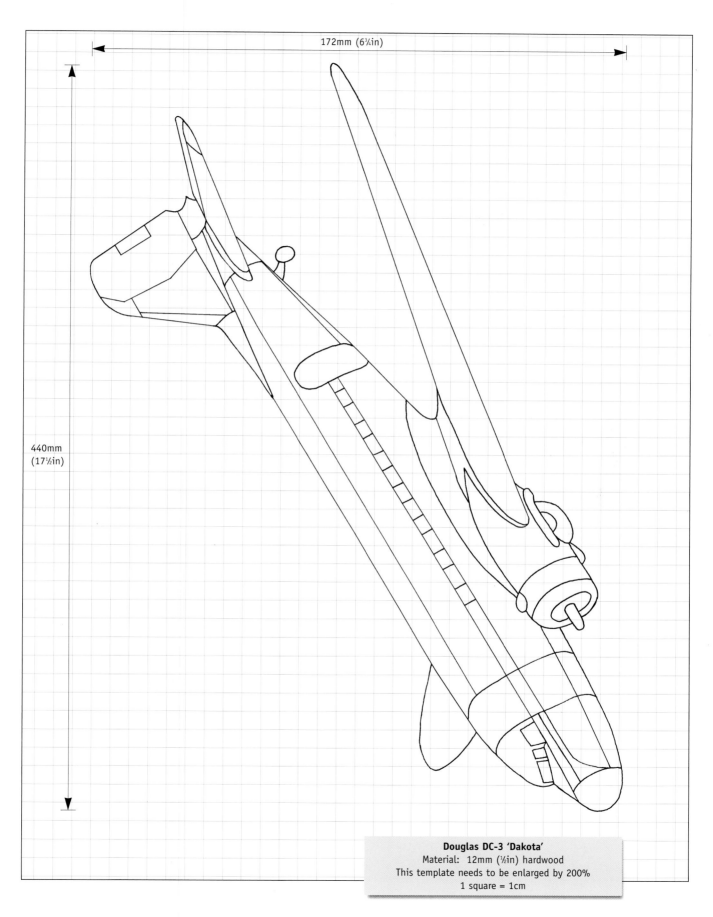

172mm (6¾in)

440mm
(17½in)

Douglas DC-3 'Dakota'
Material: 12mm (½in) hardwood
This template needs to be enlarged by 200%
1 square = 1cm

D H Comet

This intarsia design is based upon the D H Comet and executed in the colours of the Royal Air Force Transport Command. Alongside the other aircraft panel designs in this book, it provides the scrollsawer with a striking contrast of old and new.

The model has a backing panel in the approximate shape of a sliced-off oval. The aircraft itself is cut from a sandwich of two different thicknesses of ply, and includes a repetition of the oval back panel in the

aircraft's mounting. The aircraft is cut from 6mm (¼in) birch ply and sandwiched with a further sheet of 4mm (⅛in) birch ply so that it stands proud from the oval back panel.

To add drama, the wings and part of the tailplane of the aircraft extend out beyond the confines of the oval mount – almost as though taking off from it. I have not actually cut out the cockpit detail due to size limitations and have instead added the markings with a fine-point permanent marker pen.

Begin the project by marking out and cutting the base panel. For the original model shown here, I used a piece of 6mm (¼in) hardwood salvaged from an old piece of

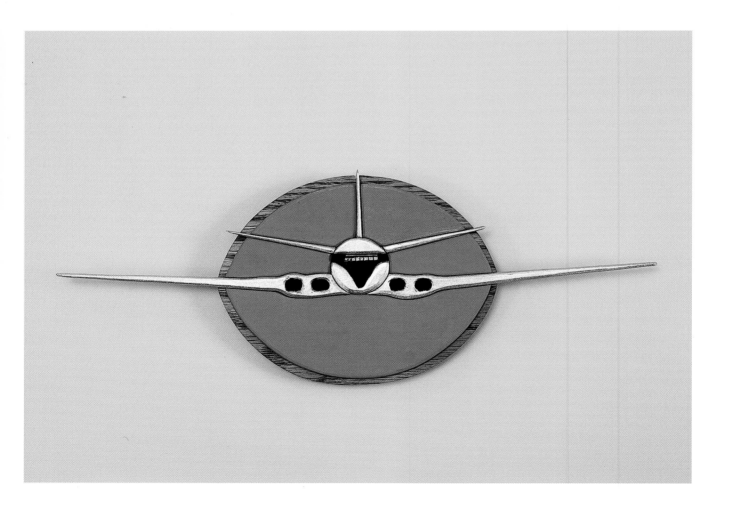

Making up a sandwich of a piece of birch ply to form the aircraft and the mount for the sky

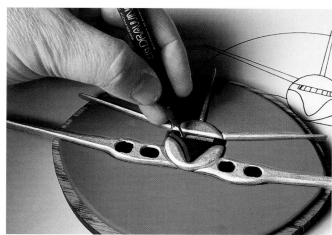

Marking in the cockpit detail with a fine-point permanent marker pen

furniture. First, I cleaned it with an orbital sander and then applied a coat of satin varnish for a nice sheen.

Next make up a sandwich of a piece of 6mm (¼in) and 4mm (⅛in) birch ply of the same size. Stick down the cutting pattern and cut out all the individual pieces, but, for the moment, leave the shaping operations.

Retain the 6mm (¼in) ply pieces of the aircraft itself and discard the rest. Similarly, retain the 4mm (⅛in) pieces for the mount

for the sky background. Now you have the right pieces, you can shape them before making up the completed project.

Next paint the aircraft in your choice of livery; it doesn't have to be the same as mine. Mount the painted aircraft onto its base panel with glue, taking care to position the aircraft in the centre accurately.

Using the marker pen, add the cockpit details by referring to the cutting pattern and, to complete, apply a coat of satin varnish.

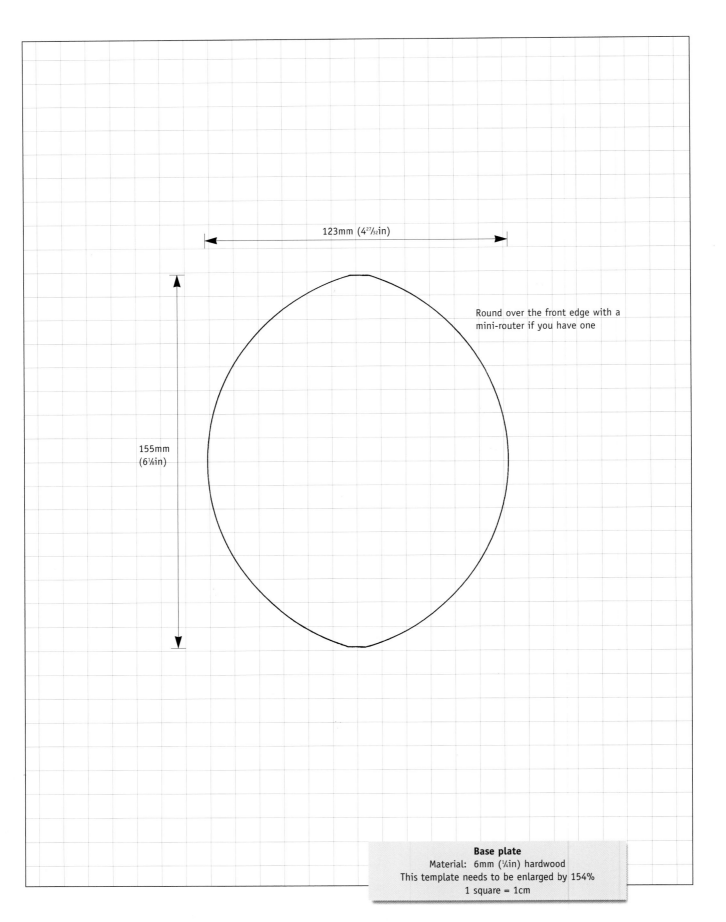

123mm (4²⁷⁄₃₂in)

155mm
(6⅛in)

Round over the front edge with a
mini-router if you have one

Base plate
Material: 6mm (¼in) hardwood
This template needs to be enlarged by 154%
1 square = 1cm

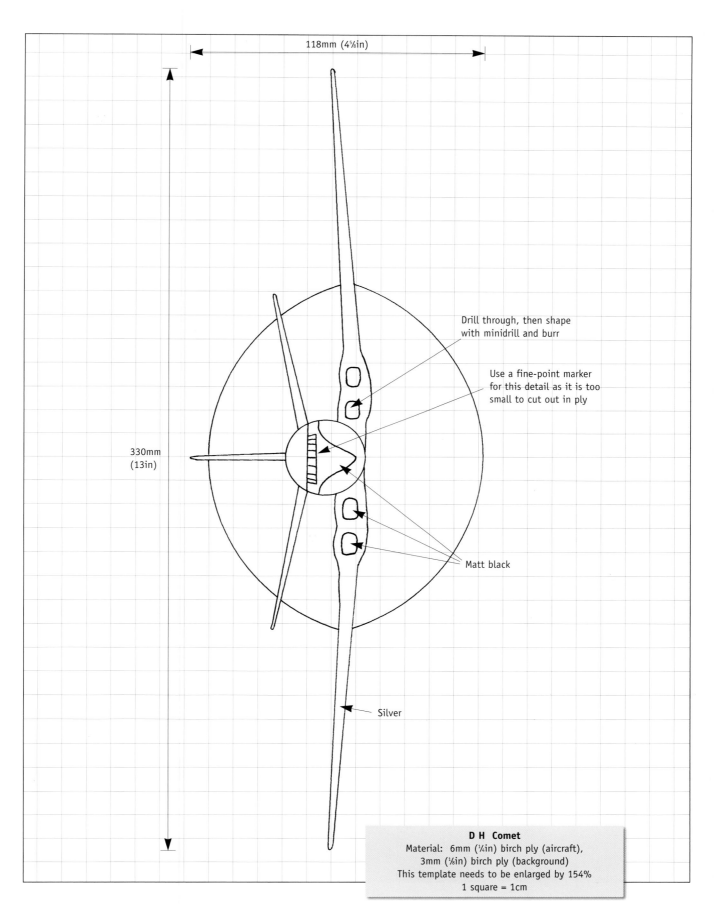

118mm (4⅝in)

330mm
(13in)

Drill through, then shape
with minidrill and burr

Use a fine-point marker
for this detail as it is too
small to cut out in ply

Matt black

Silver

D H Comet
Material: 6mm (¼in) birch ply (aircraft),
3mm (⅛in) birch ply (background)
This template needs to be enlarged by 154%
1 square = 1cm

Windmill

The windmill is very straightforward to make and delightful to hang on your wall. Before you begin cutting and shaping, make a spare copy of the cutting pattern to lay out the individual parts as you work; this enables you to accurately centre the design onto its base.

The windmill shown here was painted in natural colours and, so as not to detract from the image, the base panel was finished simply in natural wood stain. You can, of course, choose your own colour combinations and finish for a unique project.

Begin by sticking down the cutting pattern onto your sheet of 4mm (1/16in) ply to make up the windmill itself. Cut out the individual pieces, shape and then decorate them. Once complete, stick the pieces down onto a backing panel as shown in the template. Next trim the 4mm (1/16in) ply backing panel to the dimensions given and touch up the edges with your chosen colours before positioning the picture onto its base panel.

While it is pleasing to keep this design simple, if you wish, you may add a frame, too.

Using a flexible sanding pad to clean up the more intricate parts of the design

Windmill plaque
Material: Base 12mm (½in) ply, backing panel 4mm
(¹⁄₁₆in) ply, overlay 4mm (¹⁄₁₆in) ply
This template needs to be enlarged by 143%
1 square = 1cm

Horus, the Sun God

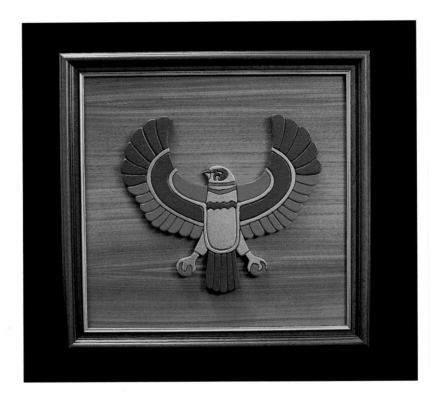

The art and culture of Pharaonic Egypt is very popular, making this an appealing project for those scrollsawers with an interest in ancient history.

This design is inspired by the ancient Egyptian sun god, Horus, a falcon-like god whose image is found in many of the Royal tombs in the Valley of the Kings, and upon which our present-day horoscope is founded. The original model has been considerably simplified to make it a reasonable proposition as an intarsia design, and the colour combination is authentic, based as it is on colour photographs of actual wall paintings.

No details have been provided for a backing board for this pattern so that you can make your own choice. I bonded the original to a sheet of 6mm (¼in) birch ply and mounted it in a square frame, which I think suits the design well, but there is no hard-and-fast rule.

The design was cut from 9mm (⅜in) hardwood but you may also use ply or MDF, whatever you have to hand, particularly if you are working to a budget and have the opportunity to recycle old pieces of furniture. If possible, it is best to avoid waste and to use what is, after all, well-seasoned, good quality wood.

Sticking down the cutting pattern

Cutting away extraneous material to make the pattern ready for final cutting

Cutting out the elements of the design

To begin, make up a cutting pattern to the final size of your plaque, and trace the outline onto the centre of a sheet of paper large enough to completely cover your chosen backing board. It is a good idea, too, to cut out a spare pattern. Cut out the traced outline so you are left with a falcon-shaped hole in the paper. Now place the cutout into position on the backing board, and secure it with masking tape. This will act as a guide for accurately positioning the falcon pieces once you have cut them out and painted them.

Continue cutting out the individual pieces of the design, using your spare cutting pattern to position the pieces as you work. Once you get to the smaller parts of the design, it is a good idea to fit a false saw table on top of your usual saw table.

To make a false saw table, simply take a piece of scrap ply or MDF and run it into position by sawing down it with the existing blade in your scrollsaw so that there is no gap

Using a false saw table to avoid losing small parts on the floor

around the blade. Once you have the wood, ply or MDF in place, secure it with some adhesive tape. This arrangement will reduce the gap between the blade and saw table so that, as each small part is cut, you won't lose pieces through the saw table onto the floor.

Once you have all the individual pieces cut out, round off the display sides with a drum sander attached to the chuck of your minidrill, and hold it in place with a bench clamp. By doing this, you leave both hands free to control the workpiece.

Once sanded, decorate the pieces by following the colours suggested here on my model or to your preference. Many of the original ancient examples of this design are executed to stunning effect in gold and this would make a very striking alternative finish, particularly against a dark blue backing panel.

If you wish, complete your piece as I have by bonding it to a backing board and either having it framed or frame it yourself.

Using the miniature drum sander to shape the pieces

Using a burr in the minidrill to accentuate the saw kerfs used to denote the features

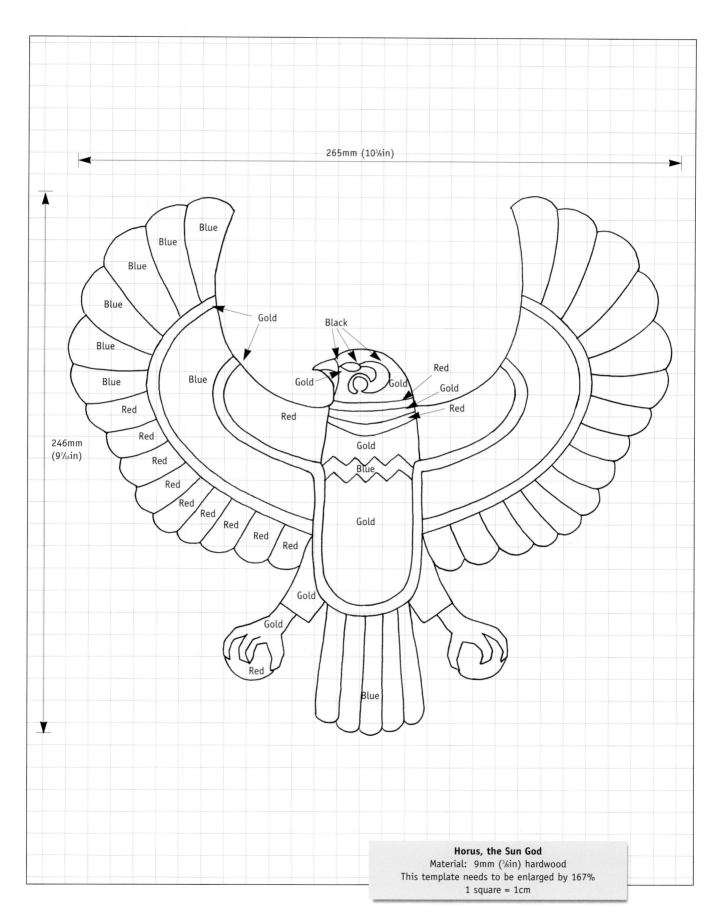

265mm (10⅜in)

246mm (9⁷⁄₁₆in)

Blue
Blue
Blue
Blue
Blue
Blue
Blue
Blue
Red
Red
Red
Red
Red
Red
Red
Red
Red

Gold
Blue

Black
Gold
Red
Gold
Gold
Red
Red
Gold
Blue

Gold

Gold
Gold
Red

Blue

Horus, the Sun God
Material: 9mm (⅜in) hardwood
This template needs to be enlarged by 167%
1 square = 1cm

Stephenson's Rocket

This is the classic steam locomotive, being one of the first and most famous if its kind. In order to accentuate the moving parts that this pattern involves, the couplings and axles for example, I have drilled small holes with a minidrill and inserted brass panel pins for added decorative effect. There are quite a few difficult parts to cut and shape in this project, so if you have the use of a minidrill with a tapered burr and a miniature half-round file, these will prove extremely useful. The wheels are particularly tricky, especially those with spokes. Even the minimum of saw tear-out can be problematic without breaking one or more of these, so take a great deal of care handling these parts.

First, make up the backing panel, then the cutting pattern for the locomotive and a spare copy to help you lay out your pieces in the correct order. Next cut out all the locomotive parts, and drill the small pilot holes for the brass pins. Unless you have very short pins, either increase the thickness of the backing panel or use a cut-off disc on your minidrill to reduce the pins so that they are flush with the surface of the backing panel. You can also use miniature end-cutters for this purpose.

Once you have cut and shaped all the parts and drilled the pilot holes, begin assembly onto the backing panel by removing part of the cutting pattern and using this as a guide for sticking the first pieces into position. Once the glue has dried, you have an accurate reference to locate and glue down the remaining pieces. Allow the glue to dry thoroughly and then add the brass pins.

All that remains is to apply a coat of protective varnish to prevent the brass pins from oxidizing and to hang the finished plaque.

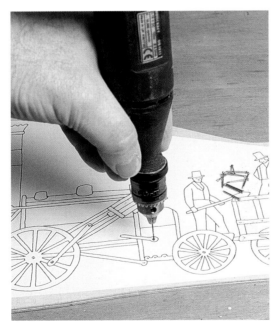

Drilling the pilot holes for the brass pins before cutting out

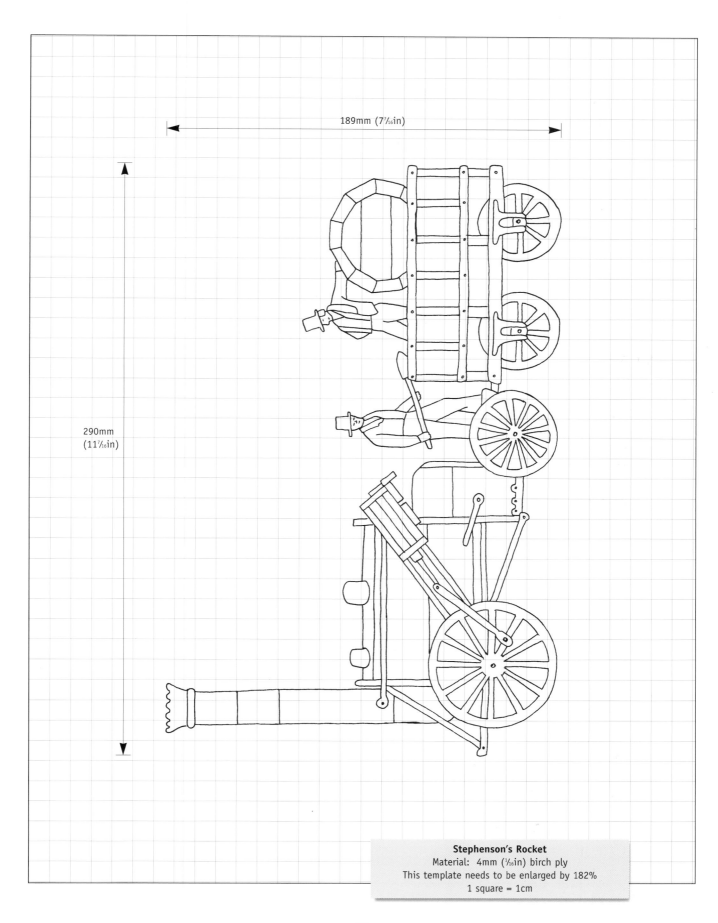

189mm (7⁷⁄₁₆in)

290mm
(11⁷⁄₁₆in)

Stephenson's Rocket
Material: 4mm (⅛₆in) birch ply
This template needs to be enlarged by 182%
1 square = 1cm

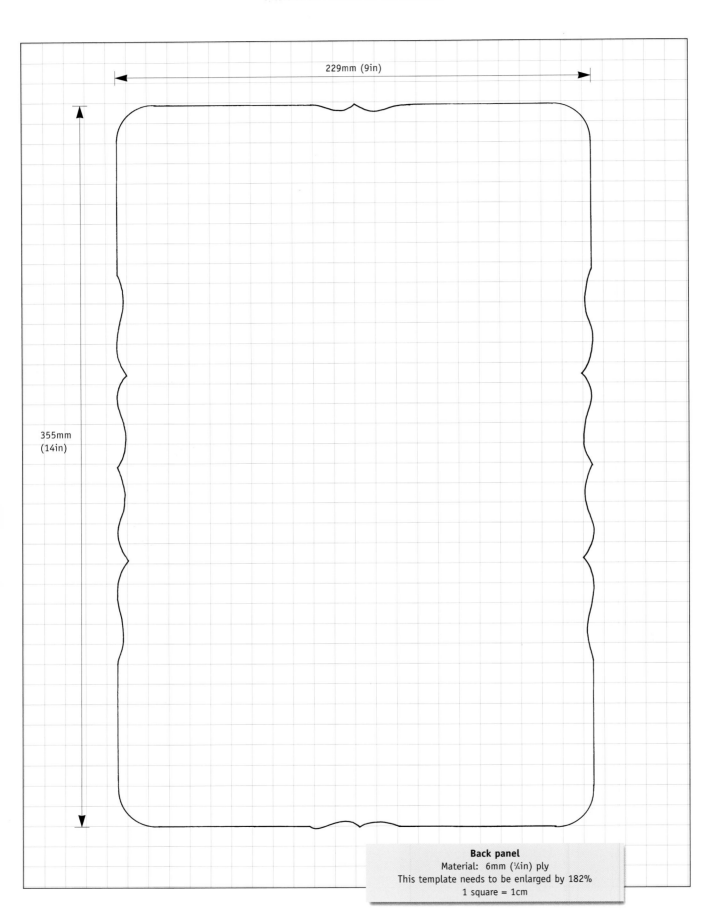

229mm (9in)

355mm
(14in)

Back panel
Material: 6mm (¼in) ply
This template needs to be enlarged by 182%
1 square = 1cm

Heraldic eagle

This is a great project for the classically inclined, or those who have an entrance hall, front door or gate that is otherwise lacking sufficient grandeur. I have not provided a pattern for the back panel which I have fashioned into a shield shape as there are so many variations and sizes that it is best to leave it to personal preference. If you wish, you might mount it in a simple, rectangular frame which would also make an impressive vehicle for display.

Begin by making up a cutting pattern and a spare copy to lay out the pieces in order. Next decide on the shape of your back panel and cut this out before embarking on the cutting operations. The original model was made from a piece of 6mm (¼in) ply and stained with dark oak wood stain which lends the shield an authentic medieval appearance and nicely complements the gold and red elements.

There are quite a few saw kerf cuts to be made on this pattern. To accentuate the pieces as you shape them, use a minidrill with a tapered burr attached, and run it along the

kerf cut, rounding it so that it looks like the edges of the individual pieces of the eagle.

Next, cut out and shape the parts of the eagle, laying them carefully on the spare cutting pattern as you work. Once you have the complete set cut and shaped, decorate them in the colours of your choice or follow the colour combination shown here, using metallic grey to work the eyes.

To position the finished eagle design correctly onto your back panel, cut away the tail section of the eagle from the spare cutting pattern, together with all the extraneous paper, and place it centred on your backing panel. Glue the tail part in place and you have a point of reference for all the other parts of the eagle. Once complete, you need only make use of further treatment if you want to mount it outside the house, in which case apply a couple of coats of good quality weatherproof varnish.

Using a tapered burr in the minidrill to delineate the kerf cuts which accentuate the eagle's features

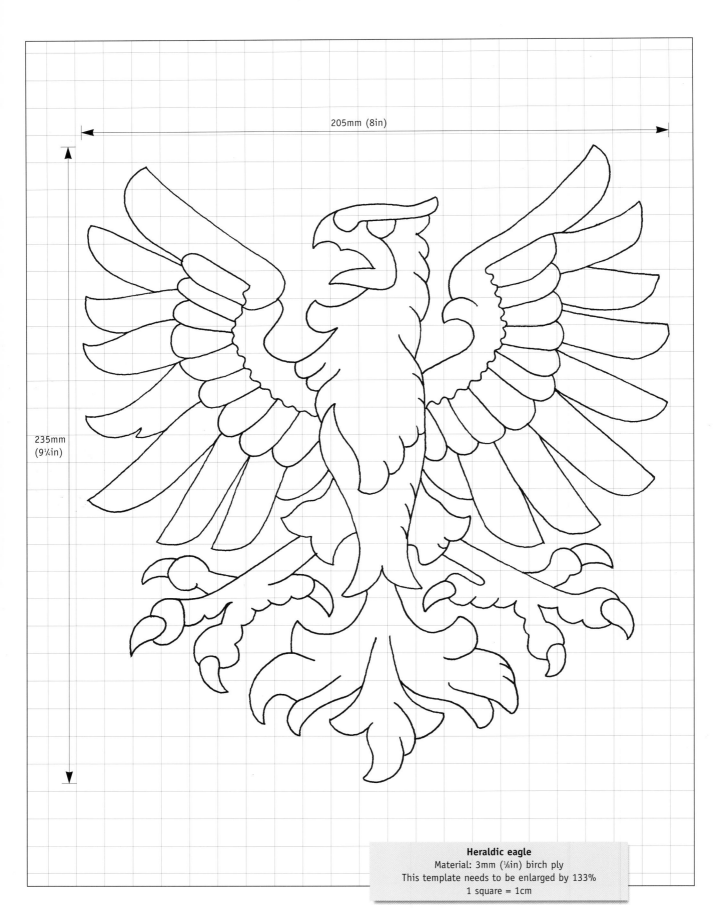

205mm (8in)

235mm (9¼in)

Heraldic eagle
Material: 3mm (⅛in) birch ply
This template needs to be enlarged by 133%
1 square = 1cm

Geometric I

This abstract geometric design works well executed in contemporary colours and offset slightly on its back panel to give a less uniform feel to the finished item. As I've mentioned elsewhere, don't forget to cut a spare cutting pattern as many of the parts are identical and only differ in the extent of how accurately they are cut – and, of course, you want them to fit together properly again.

Make up the base panel so that it is approximately 25mm (1in) greater than the overall size of the design, then cut out and shape all the parts that make up the design. Decorate the pieces in the colours I've used here or your own combination.

To finish, either centre the finished design onto the back panel, or maintain the slightly offset manner of my original. To do this, slightly lower the design off-centre until you achieve the desired effect. You can hang the piece as it is or, if you wish, frame it simply.

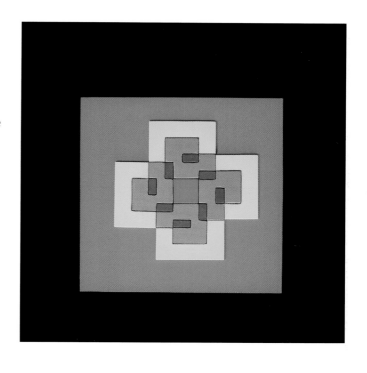

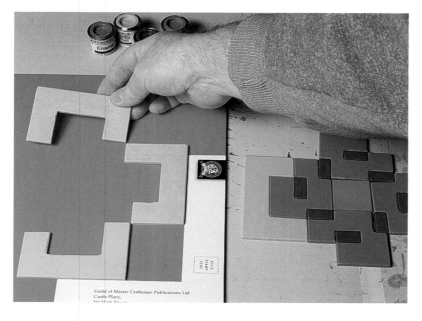

Using a card template to position the pieces onto the back panel, slightly offset from the centre for an abstract feel

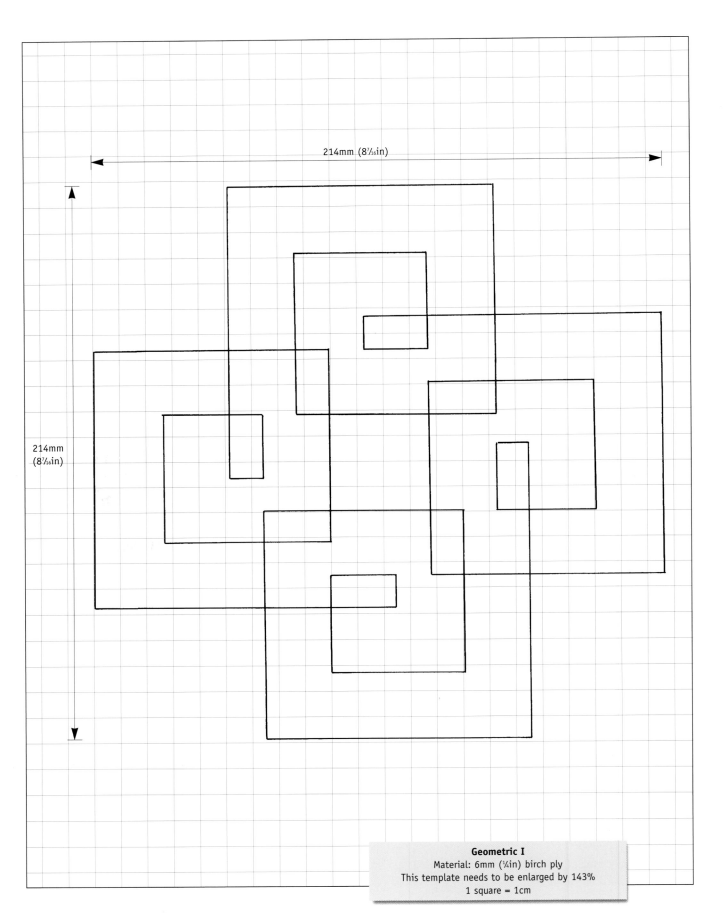

214mm (8⁷⁄₁₆in)

214mm
(8⁷⁄₁₆in)

Geometric I
Material: 6mm (¼in) birch ply
This template needs to be enlarged by 143%
1 square = 1cm

Geometric II

This is an intarsia pattern influenced by one of those optical illusion drawings based on obscure mathematical formulae. The finished panel gives the illusion of three separate cubes interlocking. In true intarsia fashion, the project is created with individually worked pieces which cast shadows across each other, reinforcing the illusion of depth in the completed design.

This is a straightforward project. It is made from a small piece of 6mm (¼in) birch ply and, quite simply, you just 'cut 'em, shape 'em and stick 'em' back together. Once complete, add a coat of satin varnish and mount on the wall with a picture hook.

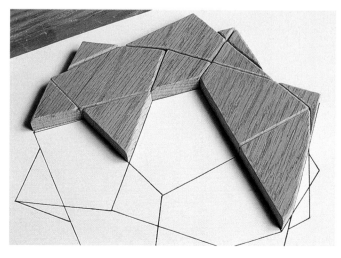

Positioning the geometric cutouts on the spare cutting pattern to help you lay them out for assembly

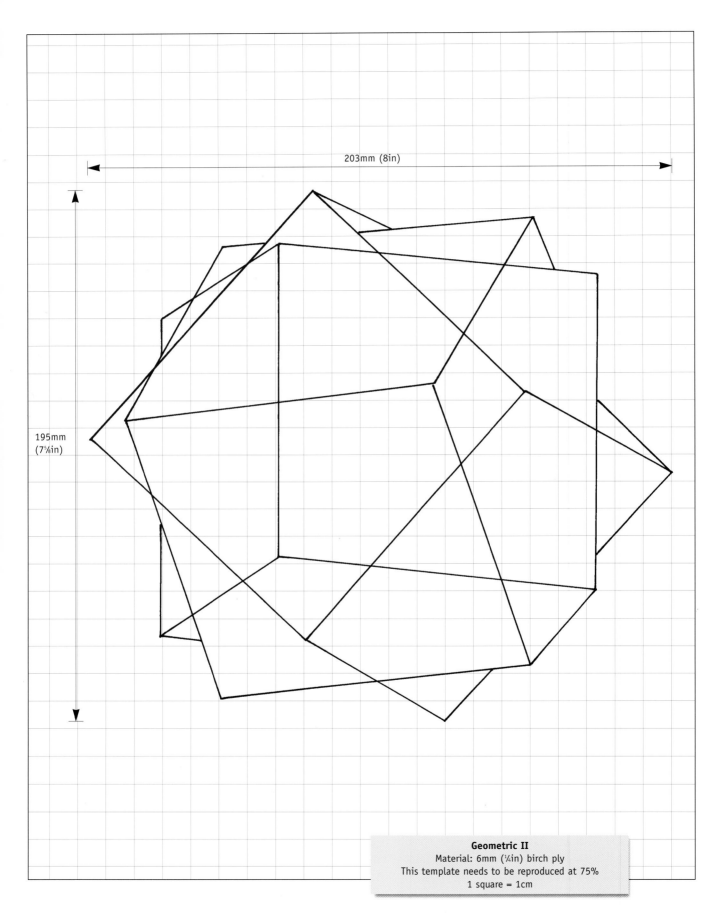

203mm (8in)

195mm
(7⅝in)

Geometric II
Material: 6mm (¼in) birch ply
This template needs to be reproduced at 75%
1 square = 1cm

Stonehenge

A monument shrouded in the mysteries of the past, that is Stonehenge, and it renews its mystical status every mid-summer solstice when the Druids make their pilgrimage. While it is virtually impossible to see the sunrise through the stones of Stonehenge these days – the weather usually isn't up to it – it is easy to illuminate the scene with sunlight in this intarsia design.

My original model is made from a sheet of 6mm (¼in) birch ply on a base of the same material. Keeping the selection of colours to a minimum and and the wood in its natural state, allows the scene to look fresh, as

Laying out the individual pieces of cutout onto the backing panel in order to check the fit

though the weather really is going to hold out. By working out the design on wood, you can position the sun exactly where you like, too.

Begin by mounting your cutting pattern onto the ply with Spray Mount adhesive, and cut out all the parts. Shape each piece individually and then apply your chosen wood dyes. Of course, alternatively, you can use other finishes, including watercolour or acrylics paints, depending on your desired effect.

To finish, glue the individual pieces of the scene in place on the backing panel and then mount or frame as you wish.

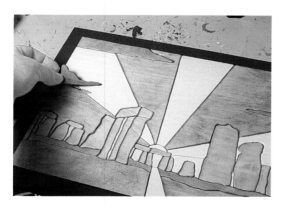

Adding the final piece to the intarsia Stonehenge – a very satisfying moment

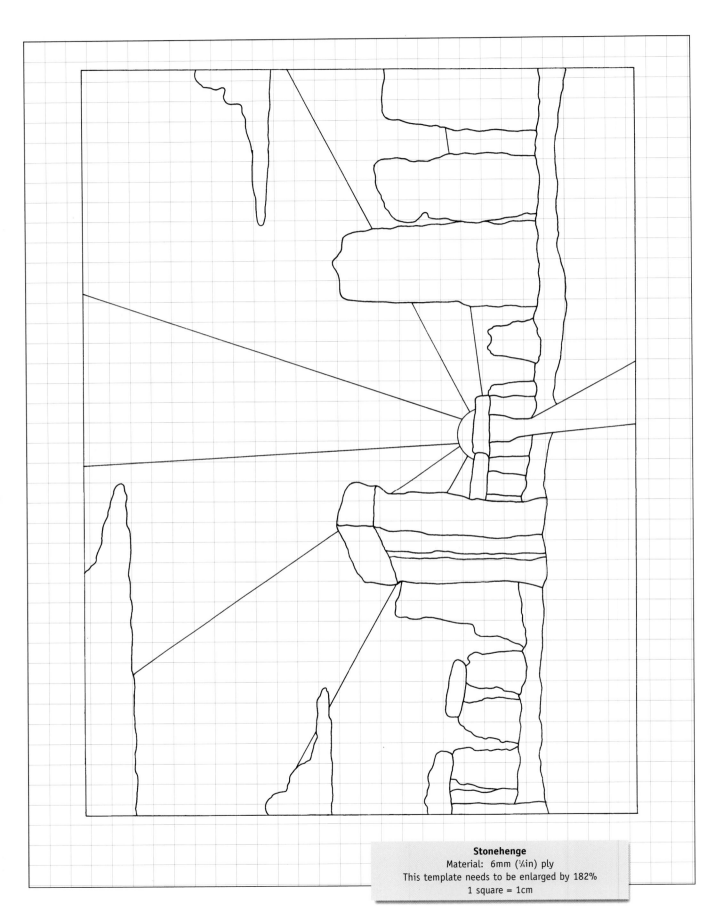

Stonehenge
Material: 6mm (¼in) ply
This template needs to be enlarged by 182%
1 square = 1cm

Hawker Fury I

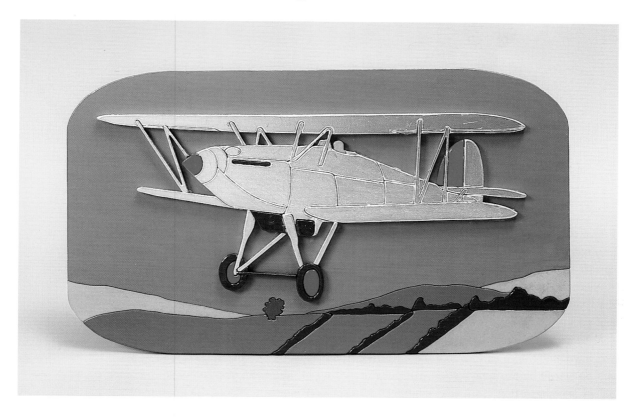

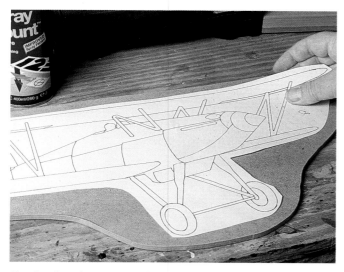

The aircraft cutting pattern stuck down in position ready for cutting out

This design makes use of a double layer of intarsia to make the Hawker Fury I stand out impressively. The upper part of the background layer, where the aircraft is positioned, is left free of elaboration as a contrast to the aerial view of fields and hedgerows below. Although the sizes for the panels given are fairly large, a small scrollsaw can ably cope with the scale of this design.

The design for the biplane shown here has been made from 6mm (¼in) MDF, which is quite adequate. By all means use an alternative, thinner material if you wish, but it may prove difficult to handle in terms of mechanical strength, so do bear this in mind.

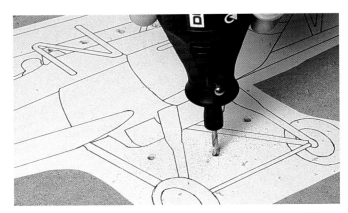

Using the minidrill to make starter holes for the internal cutouts on the pattern. These cut away parts reveal the background through the gaps

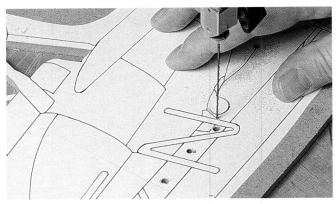

Carefully cutting out the struts and other small parts on the scrollsaw

I have painted my original model, and you may copy it or select your own colour combination.

Begin by making up the cutting patterns in the finished size you want to make the project and stick them into position. It is probably best to begin with the background panel so you have a reference as to where the aircraft will be placed on the final picture. Cut out the pieces and shape them with your minidrill, decorate them and stick them together on a backing sheet. The template supplied shows where to position the aircraft once you have assembled the background.

Next cut out the aircraft, paying attention to the struts and other small parts as these will need a little careful handling to avoid damage. Once you have cut out and painted the aircraft parts and these are dry, lay out the parts in their correct positions onto the background panel. You can then remove each individual part of the aircraft, glue it and stick it down. Allow the glue to dry so that each remains properly affixed. By following this technique, you will have an accurate reference point for all the other parts of the aircraft.

Finally, add picture hangers behind the panel and mount your picture to a wall.

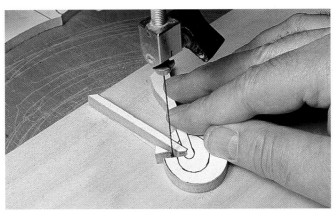

Separating the wheel parts on the scrollsaw

Laying out the aircraft components into position to check their fit

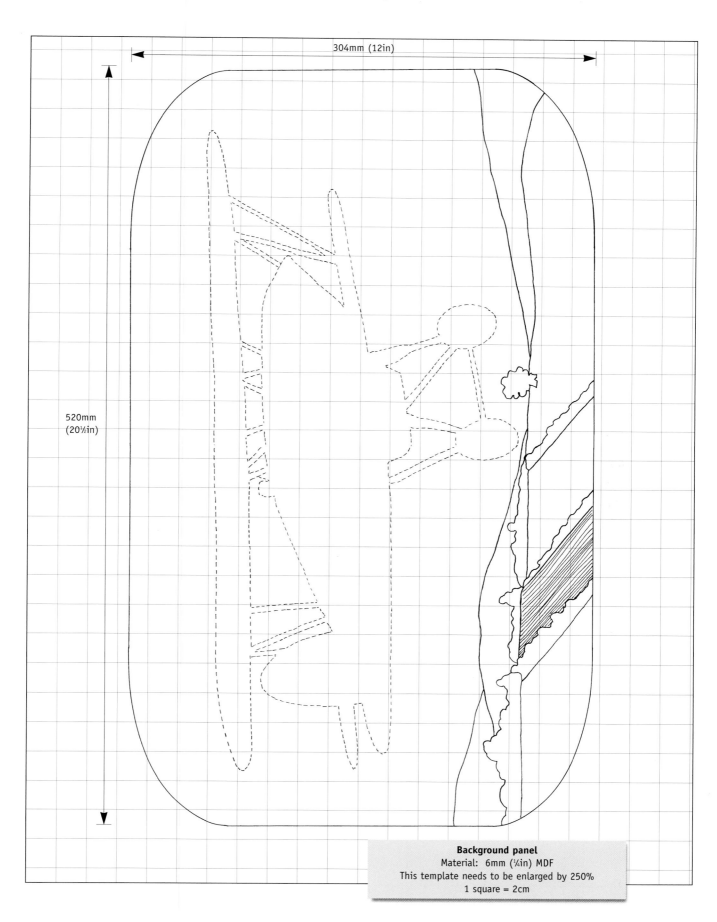

304mm (12in)

520mm
(20½in)

Background panel
Material: 6mm (¼in) MDF
This template needs to be enlarged by 250%
1 square = 2cm

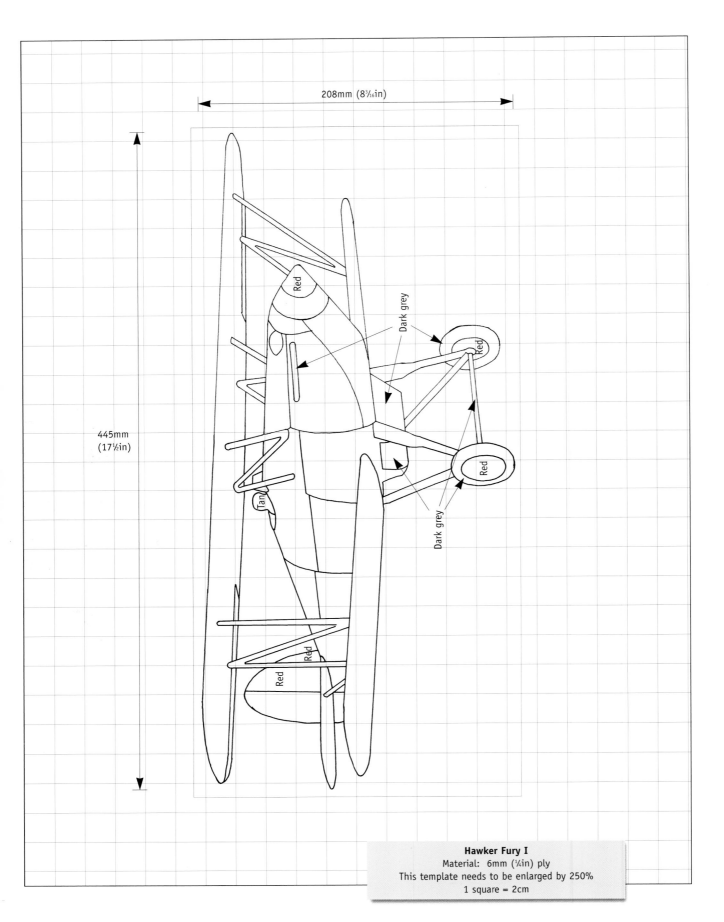

208mm (8³⁄₁₆in)

445mm
(17½in)

Red

Dark grey

Red

Dark grey

Red

Tan

Red

Red

Red

Hawker Fury I
Material: 6mm (¼in) ply
This template needs to be enlarged by 250%
1 square = 2cm

Moose at sunset

This dramatic design depicts a fine animal, executed in silhouette. The project calls for some careful cutting as the moose and sky details are quite intricate. The cutting out itself is not a problem, but you should handle the individual pieces with care as they have little mechanical strength, particularly during shaping, decorating and gluing into position.

This project consists of the intarsia, a backing panel, an overlay and a thin piece of plywood inserted between the intarsia and backing panel so that it aligns with the branch-effect frame. All the parts in the original model were cut from 4mm (⅛in) birch ply, which gives a finer finish than cheaper grades, and it is stronger too.

To begin, cut out the backing panel and the piece you intend to insert between the intarsia and the backing panel. Glue and then clamp these securely together and wait for the glue to dry thoroughly while you turn to the intarsia picture itself.

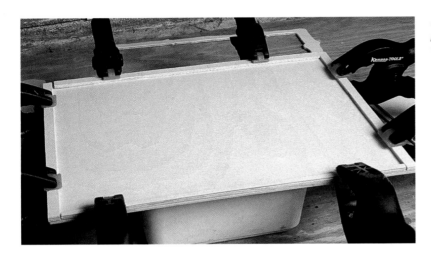

*Clamping the in-between
pieces of ply in position
while the glue dries*

*Using a burr in the minidrill
to shape the more intricate
parts of the design*

Stick down your cutting pattern to the picture panel and, once in place, cut out all the parts. In the small, intricate areas where you cannot shape with your drum sander, use the minidrill fitted with a tapered burr instead; this will manage nicely. Take care not to let the drill run away over the parts concerned to avoid damage.

Once all the intarsia elements have been cut and shaped, decorate with brightly coloured acrylic or enamel paints for a dramatic sunset. When the paint is dry, stick the intarsia parts into position. You will, of course, have the thin piece of in-between ply as a guide for positioning the pieces accurately, so this should not be a problem. Once you have completed this part of the operation, stick down the branch-effect frame and leave to dry thoroughly.

Finally, add some picture eye hooks, wire to the back and mount to a wall.

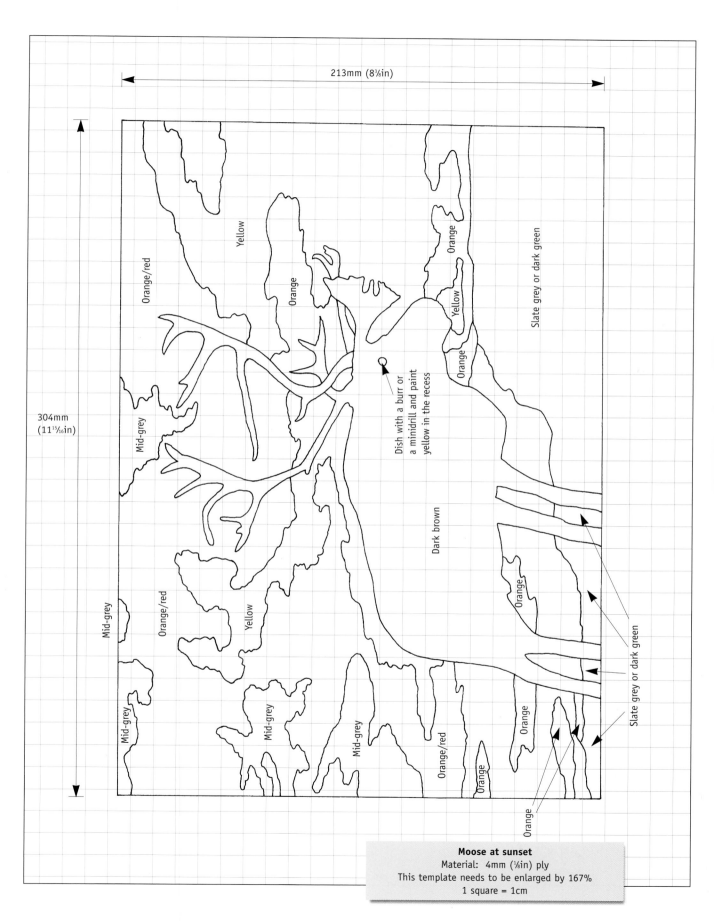

Moose at sunset
Material: 4mm (⅛in) ply
This template needs to be enlarged by 167%
1 square = 1cm

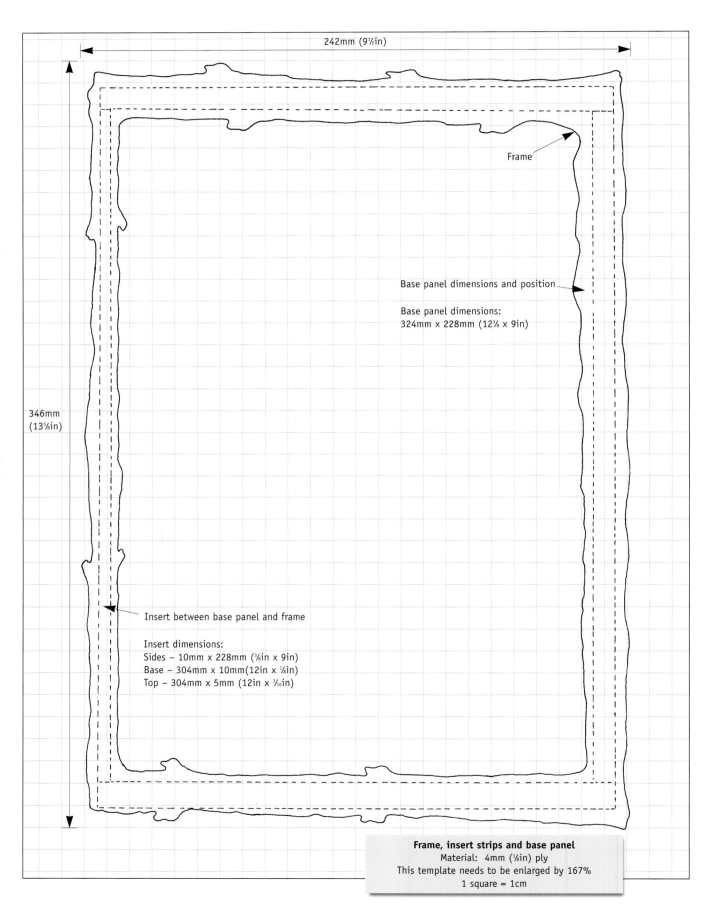

242mm (9½in)

Frame

Base panel dimensions and position

Base panel dimensions:
324mm x 228mm (12⅜ x 9in)

346mm
(13⅝in)

Insert between base panel and frame

Insert dimensions:
Sides – 10mm x 228mm (⅜in x 9in)
Base – 304mm x 10mm(12in x ⅜in)
Top – 304mm x 5mm (12in x ³⁄₁₆in)

Frame, insert strips and base panel
Material: 4mm (⅛in) ply
This template needs to be enlarged by 167%
1 square = 1cm

American clipper

This design is my own interpretation of the elegant nineteenth-century American clipper ships. The composition is made up of two intarsia panels, one for the sea and sky, the wind seeming to billow through the sails, and the other for the ship itself. The intarsia pieces are mounted onto a back panel which provides an extra dimension and stylish finish to the project.

While the gun ports on the hull of the ship are included on the cutting pattern, they are rather too small to cut accurately, so once cutting and shaping is complete, I have chosen to paint them using the cutting pattern as a positional guide. As always, it is best to make a spare copy of the cutting pattern to aid assembly of the individual parts at this stage.

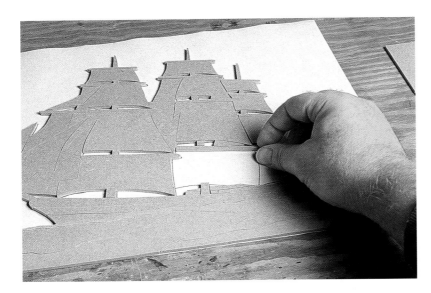

Laying out the pieces as they are cut onto a spare cutting pattern

Using a coat of gilt wax to make the border around the back panel

Begin by cutting a piece of ply large enough for the back panel to frame the intarsia. Mark the position for the picture, taking care to ensure it is centred accurately. By way of enhancement, for the model shown, I applied a coat of gilt wax to the border to enliven the scene.

Having attended to the back panel, turn your attention to the the sea/sky and ship panels. For the former, cut out the pieces, shape them, decorate to your preference, then glue them firmly into position on the backing board. Next, the ship. As before, cut out, shape and paint the ship, then carefully position the pieces into their correct locations and glue onto the sky panel.

Finally, frame and hang your fine American clipper on the wall.

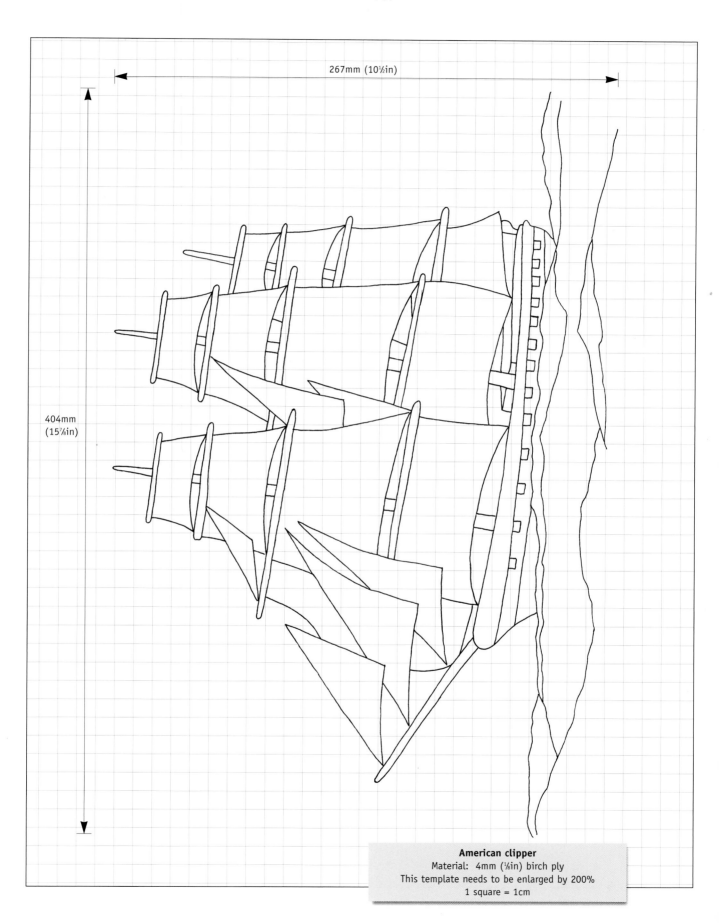

267mm (10½in)

404mm
(15⅞in)

American clipper
Material: 4mm (⅛in) birch ply
This template needs to be enlarged by 200%
1 square = 1cm

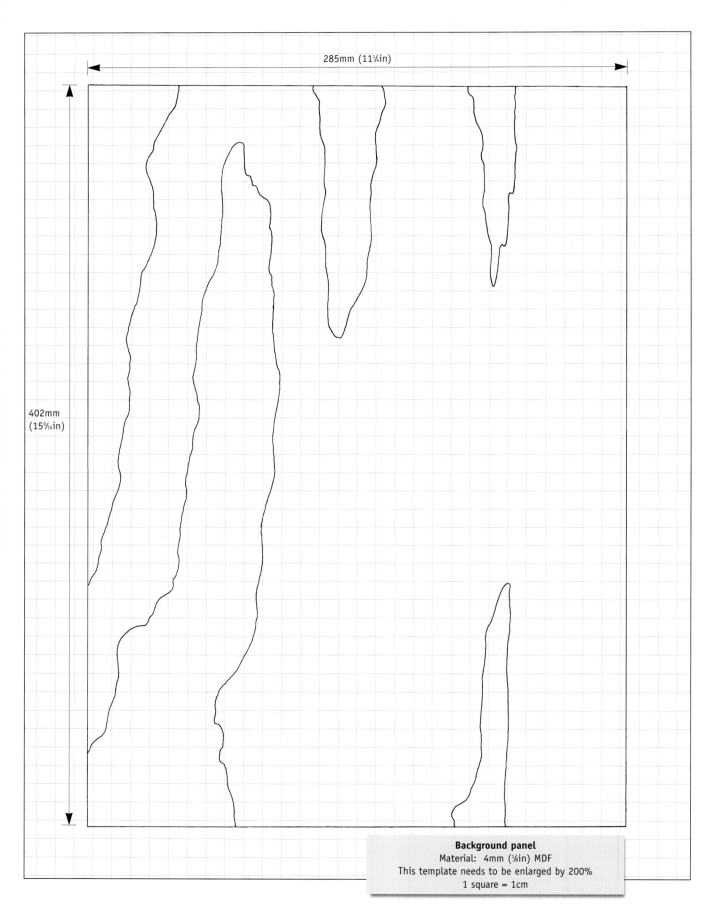

285mm (11¼in)

402mm
(15⁹⁄₁₆in)

Background panel
Material: 4mm (⅛in) MDF
This template needs to be enlarged by 200%
1 square = 1cm

1888 Benz

This intarsia design depicting a vintage Benz motor car has been conceived as a silhouette of light birch ply on a dark wood background. I made the back panel from hardwood, a piece that had a very pleasing grain and happened to be just the right size.

I rounded off the corners in simple fashion so that the overall size was approximately 25mm (1in) or so larger than the outline of the car itself.

Take care when cutting out the Benz as there are a number of very delicate, intricate parts. This is the main reason for using ply rather than a thin sheet of wood as the former has greater mechanical strength.

My model is more of an impressionistic representation than strictly historically accurate, mainly because some of the parts would otherwise have been very difficult to cut out and shape, threatening to compromise the integrity of the material. So, with apologies to Mr Benz, it still looks very nice indeed. As always, make a spare cutting pattern to aid the assembly once the parts are individually cut out.

Beginning with the cutting pattern, carefully cut out all the parts and, using first the drum sander and then the minidrill with a tapered burr, shape the individual parts. As you proceed, place each in its correct position

Using the minidrill to make a starter hole for cutting out a wheel on the motor car

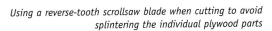

Using a reverse-tooth scrollsaw blade when cutting to avoid splintering the individual plywood parts

Using the cutting pattern to accurately centre the car on the base panel

on the spare cutting pattern to aid assembly. Once you have all the car parts cut and shaped, make up a base panel from any suitable piece of wood you have to hand or make use of another piece of ply or MDF and paint it to your preference.

To accurately position the car on its base panel, ready for gluing, begin with one of the wheels as a guide. Cut it away from the cutting pattern and centre the remaining part of the car on the base panel. Now glue the wheel in place on the base and the remaining pieces of car will fall naturally into the correct position around it.

To complete, add one or two light coats of transparent varnish to protect the surface of the panel, and attach a couple of picture eyes and some wire to the back of the panel.

610mm (24in)

224mm
(8¹³⁄₁₆in)

1888 Benz
Material: 4mm (⅛in) birch ply
This template needs to be enlarged by 111%
1 square = 1cm

Roman merchant ship

I am very fond of ships, their development in different cultures and the myriad functions and designs. This Roman merchant ship is no exception. I have added, in restrained fashion, additional rigging to the ship for realism, but if any further were included, it would be wildly impractical to make! By making use of a small supply of ring pins from your local hobby or jewellery store, you can add sufficient rigging to make it look really effective. To fit the ring pins into place, use a minidrill with a small drill bit.

The original model was destined for an existing frame, so I adapted the cutting pattern, particularly for the area of intarsia sea that stands proud from the frame, to fit exactly inside it. If you want to frame the completed project and do not already have a frame, you can make the back panel a little larger to form a decorative mount.

Cut out all the parts for the ship, shape them in the usual way and decorate according to your own preference; I finished my model with plain wood dye.

Marking up the area of intarsia sea to fit the frame

To add rigging to your ship, it will make the job a little easier if you drill the holes and fit the ring pins in place with epoxy resin adhesive *before* actually assembling the ship onto its back panel. Once you have the ring pins in place and the adhesive has set, you are free to assemble them.

Now add the rigging. You can make this from any colour and thickness of thread, but, for my model, I chose to use beige crochet cotton; this nicely simulates the rope used on ships in the Mediterranean at this point in shipping history. Tie one end of each rigging line to its ring pin and add a small dab of glue to secure the knot. Once set, pull the line taut and secure it to the other end. Add another dab of glue to set this end, too. Continue until all the rigging is in place.

All that remains is to frame your work and mount it to the wall.

Drilling the holes for the ring pins to secure the rigging before final assembly

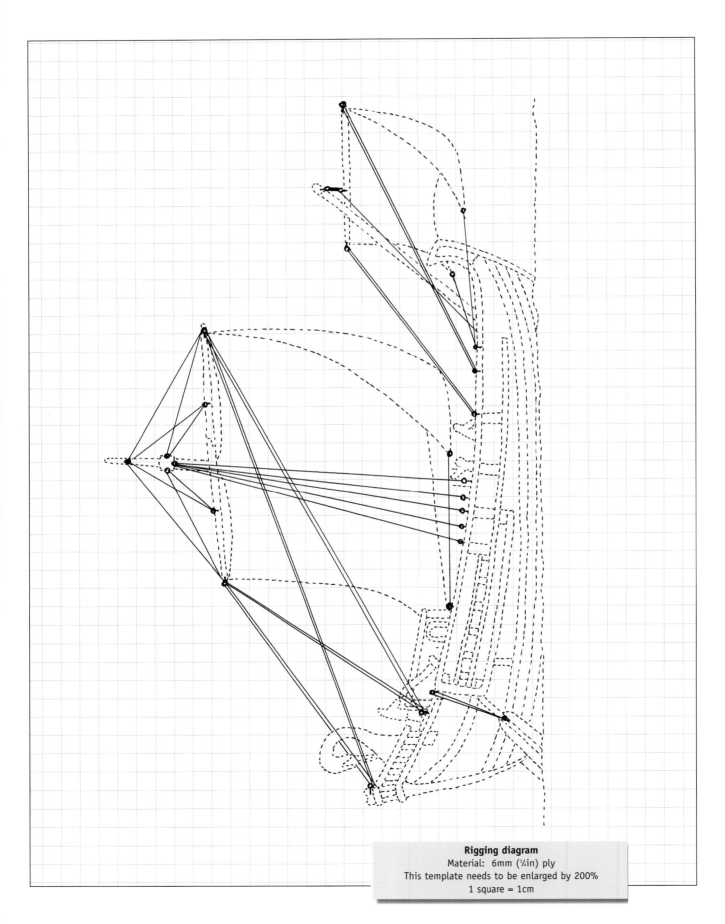

Rigging diagram
Material: 6mm (¼in) ply
This template needs to be enlarged by 200%
1 square = 1cm

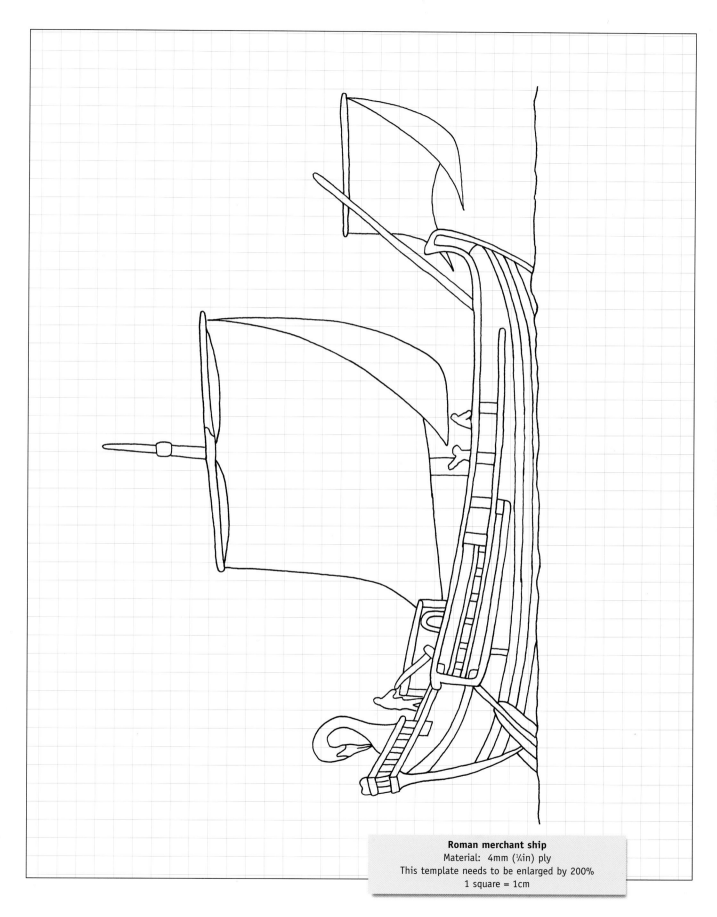

Roman merchant ship
Material: 4mm (¼in) ply
This template needs to be enlarged by 200%
1 square = 1cm

Johnson
locomotive

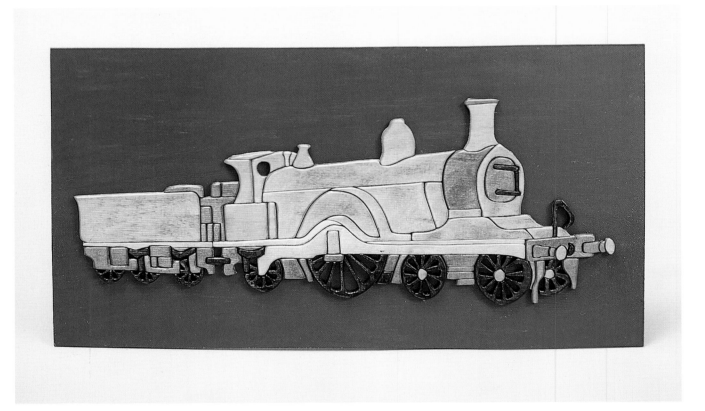

Another attractive locomotive pattern for railway buffs, based on the famous 1887 Johnson design. This one has been mounted to a back panel painted dark green as a foil to the range of natural wood dyes that I have chosen for the birch ply. I have not specified a finite size for the back panel as this will depend upon personal preference and what materials are available.

This design includes quite a large number of wheels – all with spokes – so you will need to take a great deal of care during assembly.

Laying out the pieces as they are cut from the blank panel

There are also quite a few small, intricate parts, so for cutting out, you will need to make use of your temporary saw table. In addition, you will need a minidrill fitted with a taper burr, and a miniature file is also very helpful. As always, make a spare cutting pattern for laying out the individual parts as

you cut and shape them, to aid assembly and to ensure the design is properly centred onto the backing panel.

Finally, to provide effective long-term protection for my model, I have used a couple of coats of natural wood dyes for a pleasing matt finish.

Carefully cutting out the wheels of the locomotive from the blank

Cutting the smaller pieces using a temporary saw table to avoid losing small, intricate parts through the blade hole

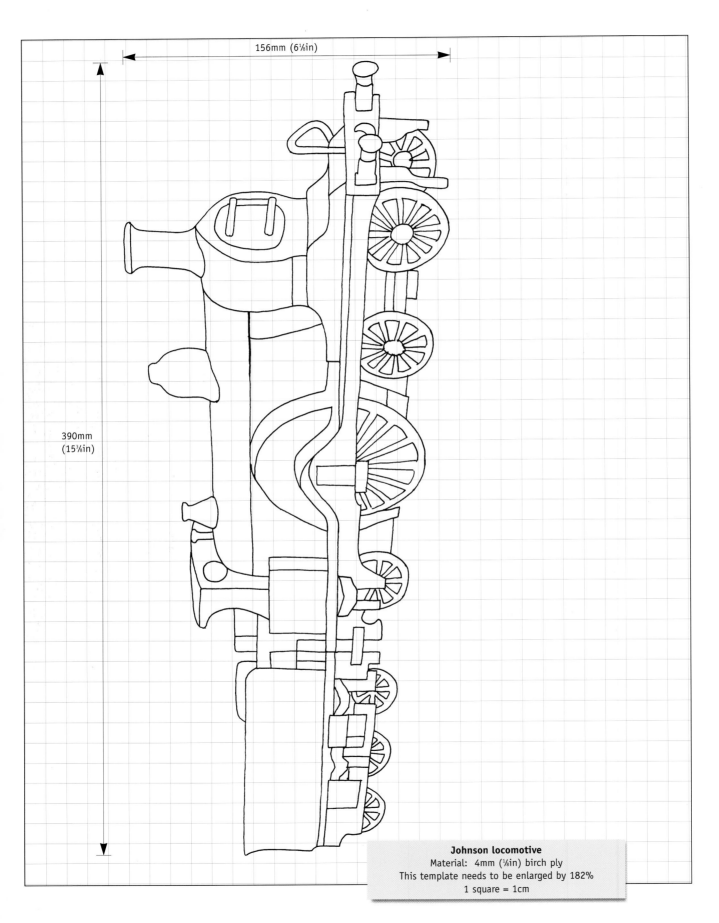

156mm (6⅛in)

390mm (15⅜in)

Johnson locomotive
Material: 4mm (⅛in) birch ply
This template needs to be enlarged by 182%
1 square = 1cm

Seventeenth-century beach scene

This design has been adapted from an engraving completed in 1690 which I find an inspiring intarsia subject.

While the techniques for this panel will be familiar by this stage, it is a complex design with a large number of intricate pieces and is, therefore, perhaps less suited to the beginner. You will find it easier to approach the project if you have a minidrill with small drill attachments and a pair of miniature pliers, preferably those with a smooth, rather than serrated, edge on the pincers. You will also find diamond-coated miniature files useful for both forward-motion

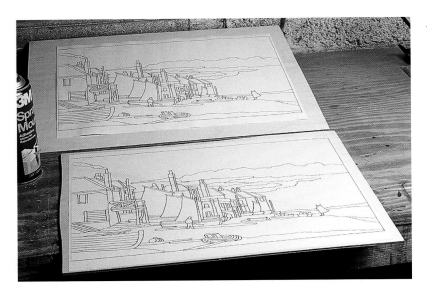

Securing the spare cutting pattern to the base panel

Handling smaller pieces with miniature pliers or tweezers

work and as a draw file as they adapt to any direction. When using the drum sander, particularly during shaping operations, handle the pieces firmly, but gently, or they may end up flying out of your hand by accident.

Make your base panel from a piece of 6mm (¼in) birch ply, about 25mm (1in) greater than the overall size of your final picture.

For my original model, I used a rosewood wood dye to stain the surface, lending the piece a pleasing matt finish, and painted the picture itself using watercolours in pastel tones. I like to use watercolour paints to finish a model as the 'wash' effect is very attractive and enables the grain of your chosen material to show through.

Once you have cut out the base panel and stained it with the rosewood dye, use a spare cutting pattern to accurately position the individual parts as they are cut and shaped. This process is absolutely essential; there are several hundred pieces to fit within an A3 size panel. Without the guidance of starter holes, many parts must be cut in sequence. Do not hurry this stage; the original shown took me about three days to complete.

Once you have cut out all the parts, and shaped and sanded them, place them into their correct positions, closing up any gaps that may have occurred as a result of sawing.

Now glue the picture into place and decorate it. Due to the character of birch ply, you will find that the surface has a tendency to soak up substantial quantities of the watercolour paint, so mix quite a bit more than you think is necessary.

The choice of colour combination is entirely your own, but it is preferable to keep the colours as realistic as possible to retain the authenticity of the scene. Whichever colours you use, decorate your chosen frame to complement them, allow the paint to dry thoroughly and then make ready to mount your beach scene onto the wall.

Applying watercolour paints to the assembled panel for a pastel finish

265mm (10⅜in)

412mm
(16⁷⁄₃₂in)

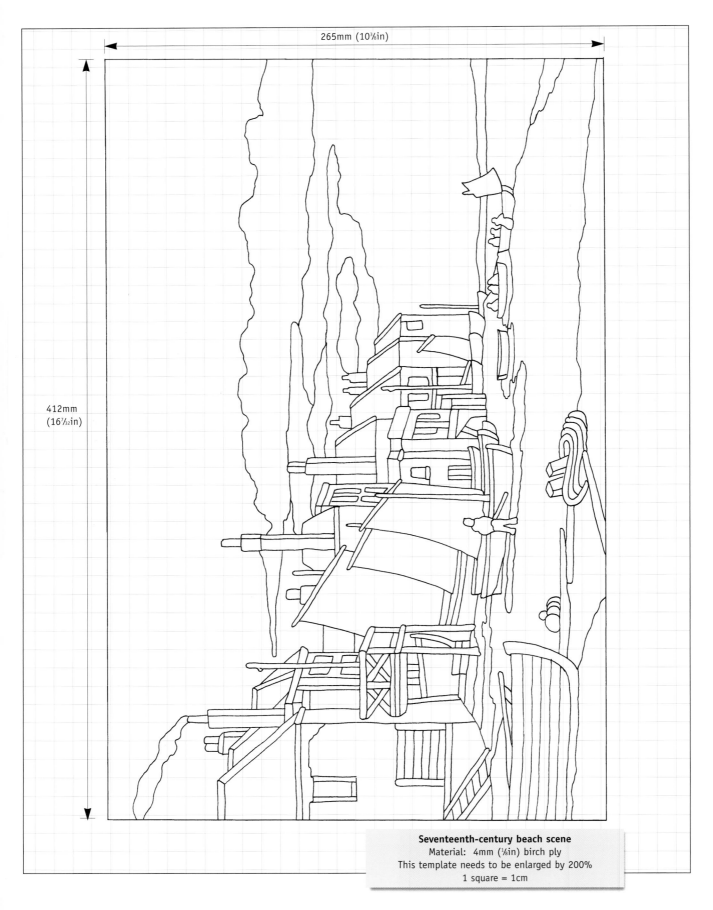

Seventeenth-century beach scene
Material: 4mm (⅛in) birch ply
This template needs to be enlarged by 200%
1 square = 1cm

Metric conversion table

inches to millimetres

inches	mm		inches	mm		inches	mm
⅛	3		9	229		30	762
¼	6		10	254		31	787
⅜	10		11	279		32	813
½	13		12	305		33	838
⅝	16		13	330		34	864
¾	19		14	356		35	889
⅞	22		15	381		36	914
1	25		16	406		37	940
1¼	32		17	432		38	965
1½	38		18	457		39	991
1¾	44		19	483		40	1016
2	51		20	508		41	1041
2½	64		21	533		42	1067
3	76		22	559		43	1092
3½	89		23	584		44	1118
4	102		24	610		45	1143
4½	114		25	635		46	1168
5	127		26	660		47	1194
6	152		27	686		48	1219
7	178		28	711		49	1245
8	203		29	737		50	1270

About the author

John Everett is a technical artist and photographer with a long-standing interest in woodwork and other crafts. He lives and works in Wales, where he produces craft kits and projects for a range of individuals and organizations, including schools and colleges.

He is a regular contributor to craft magazines, and author of four other craft books published by GMC Publications, *The Scrollsaw: Twenty Projects; Minidrill: Fifteen Projects; Glass Engraving Pattern Book* and *Practical Scrollsaw Patterns.*

TITLES AVAILABLE FROM
GMC Publications

BOOKS

WOODCARVING

The Art of the Woodcarver	GMC Publications
Carving Architectural Detail in Wood: The Classical Tradition	Frederick Wilbur
Carving Birds & Beasts	GMC Publications
Carving the Human Figure: Studies in Wood and Stone	Dick Onians
Carving Nature: Wildlife Studies in Wood	Frank Fox-Wilson
Carving Realistic Birds	David Tippey
Decorative Woodcarving	Jeremy Williams
Elements of Woodcarving	Chris Pye
Essential Woodcarving Techniques	Dick Onians
Further Useful Tips for Woodcarvers	GMC Publications
Lettercarving in Wood: A Practical Course	Chris Pye
Making & Using Working Drawings for Realistic Model Animals	Basil F. Fordham
Power Tools for Woodcarving	David Tippey
Practical Tips for Turners & Carvers	GMC Publications
Relief Carving in Wood: A Practical Introduction	Chris Pye
Understanding Woodcarving	GMC Publications
Understanding Woodcarving in the Round	GMC Publications
Useful Techniques for Woodcarvers	GMC Publications
Wildfowl Carving – Volume 1	Jim Pearce
Wildfowl Carving – Volume 2	Jim Pearce
Woodcarving: A Complete Course	Ron Butterfield
Woodcarving: A Foundation Course	Zoë Gertner
Woodcarving for Beginners	GMC Publications
Woodcarving Tools & Equipment Test Reports	GMC Publications
Woodcarving Tools, Materials & Equipment	Chris Pye

WOODTURNING

Adventures in Woodturning	David Springett
Bert Marsh: Woodturner	Bert Marsh
Bowl Turning Techniques Masterclass	Tony Boase
Colouring Techniques for Woodturners	Jan Sanders
Contemporary Turned Wood: New Perspectives in a Rich Tradition	
	Ray Leier, Jan Peters & Kevin Wallace
The Craftsman Woodturner	Peter Child
Decorative Techniques for Woodturners	Hilary Bowen
Fun at the Lathe	R.C. Bell
Illustrated Woodturning Techniques	John Hunnex
Intermediate Woodturning Projects	GMC Publications
Keith Rowley's Woodturning Projects	Keith Rowley
Practical Tips for Turners & Carvers	GMC Publications
Turning Green Wood	Michael O'Donnell
Turning Miniatures in Wood	John Sainsbury
Turning Pens and Pencils	Kip Christensen & Rex Burningham
Understanding Woodturning	Ann & Bob Phillips
Useful Techniques for Woodturners	GMC Publications
Useful Woodturning Projects	GMC Publications
Woodturning: Bowls, Platters, Hollow Forms, Vases, Vessels, Bottles, Flasks, Tankards, Plates	GMC Publications
Woodturning: A Foundation Course (New Edition)	Keith Rowley
Woodturning: A Fresh Approach	Robert Chapman
Woodturning: An Individual Approach	Dave Regester
Woodturning: A Source Book of Shapes	John Hunnex
Woodturning Jewellery	Hilary Bowen
Woodturning Masterclass	Tony Boase
Woodturning Techniques	GMC Publications
Woodturning Tools & Equipment Test Reports	GMC Publications
Woodturning Wizardry	David Springett

WOODWORKING

Advanced Scrollsaw Projects	GMC Publications
Bird Boxes and Feeders for the Garden	Dave Mackenzie
Complete Woodfinishing	Ian Hosker
David Charlesworth's Furniture-Making Techniques	David Charlesworth
The Encyclopedia of Joint Making	Terrie Noll
Furniture & Cabinetmaking Projects	GMC Publications
Furniture-Making Projects for the Wood Craftsman	GMC Publications
Furniture-Making Techniques for the Wood Craftsman	GMC Publications
Furniture Projects	Rod Wales
Furniture Restoration (Practical Crafts)	Kevin Jan Bonner
Furniture Restoration and Repair for Beginners	Kevin Jan Bonner
Furniture Restoration Workshop	Kevin Jan Bonner
Green Woodwork	Mike Abbott
Kevin Ley's Furniture Projects	Kevin Ley
Making & Modifying Woodworking Tools	Jim Kingshott
Making Chairs and Tables	GMC Publications
Making Classic English Furniture	Paul Richardson
Making Little Boxes from Wood	John Bennett
Making Screw Threads in Wood	Fred Holder
Making Shaker Furniture	Barry Jackson
Making Woodwork Aids and Devices	Robert Wearing
Mastering the Router	Ron Fox
Minidrill: Fifteen Projects	John Everett
Pine Furniture Projects for the Home	Dave Mackenzie
Practical Scrollsaw Patterns	John Everett
Router Magic: Jigs, Fixtures and Tricks to Unleash your Router's Full Potential	Bill Hylton
Routing for Beginners	Anthony Bailey
The Scrollsaw: Twenty Projects	John Everett
Sharpening: The Complete Guide	Jim Kingshott
Sharpening Pocket Reference Book	Jim Kingshott
Simple Scrollsaw Projects	GMC Publications
Space-Saving Furniture Projects	Dave Mackenzie
Stickmaking: A Complete Course	Andrew Jones & Clive George
Stickmaking Handbook	Andrew Jones & Clive George
Test Reports: *The Router* and *Furniture & Cabinetmaking*	GMC Publications
Veneering: A Complete Course	Ian Hosker
Veneering Handbook	Ian Hosker
Woodfinishing Handbook (Practical Crafts)	Ian Hosker
Woodworking with the Router: Professional Router Techniques any Woodworker can Use	Bill Hylton & Fred Matlack
The Workshop	Jim Kingshott

UPHOLSTERY

The Upholsterer's Pocket Reference Book	*David James*
Upholstery: A Complete Course (Revised Edition)	*David James*
Upholstery Restoration	*David James*
Upholstery Techniques & Projects	*David James*
Upholstery Tips and Hints	*David James*

TOYMAKING

Designing & Making Wooden Toys	*Terry Kelly*
Fun to Make Wooden Toys & Games	*Jeff & Jennie Loader*
Restoring Rocking Horses	*Clive Green & Anthony Dew*
Scrollsaw Toy Projects	*Ivor Carlyle*
Scrollsaw Toys for All Ages	*Ivor Carlyle*
Wooden Toy Projects	*GMC Publications*

DOLLS' HOUSES AND MINIATURES

1/12 Scale Character Figures for the Dolls' House	*James Carrington*
Architecture for Dolls' Houses	*Joyce Percival*
The Authentic Georgian Dolls' House	*Brian Long*
A Beginners' Guide to the Dolls' House Hobby	*Jean Nisbett*
Celtic, Medieval and Tudor Wall Hangings in 1/12 Scale Needlepoint	
	Sandra Whitehead
The Complete Dolls' House Book	*Jean Nisbett*
The Dolls' House 1/24 Scale: A Complete Introduction	*Jean Nisbett*
Dolls' House Accessories, Fixtures and Fittings	*Andrea Barham*
Dolls' House Bathrooms: Lots of Little Loos	*Patricia King*
Dolls' House Fireplaces and Stoves	*Patricia King*
Dolls' House Window Treatments	*Eve Harwood*
Easy to Make Dolls' House Accessories	*Andrea Barham*
Heraldic Miniature Knights	*Peter Greenhill*
How to Make Your Dolls' House Special: Fresh Ideas for Decorating	
	Beryl Armstrong
Make Your Own Dolls' House Furniture	*Maurice Harper*
Making Dolls' House Furniture	*Patricia King*
Making Georgian Dolls' Houses	*Derek Rowbottom*
Making Miniature Food and Market Stalls	*Angie Scarr*
Making Miniature Gardens	*Freida Gray*
Making Miniature Oriental Rugs & Carpets	*Meik & Ian McNaughton*
Making Period Dolls' House Accessories	*Andrea Barham*
Making Tudor Dolls' Houses	*Derek Rowbottom*
Making Victorian Dolls' House Furniture	*Patricia King*
Miniature Bobbin Lace	*Roz Snowden*
Miniature Embroidery for the Georgian Dolls' House	*Pamela Warner*
Miniature Embroidery for the Victorian Dolls' House	*Pamela Warner*
Miniature Needlepoint Carpets	*Janet Granger*
More Miniature Oriental Rugs & Carpets	*Meik & Ian McNaughton*
Needlepoint 1/12 Scale: Design Collections for the Dolls' House	*Felicity Price*
The Secrets of the Dolls' House Makers	*Jean Nisbett*

CRAFTS

American Patchwork Designs in Needlepoint	*Melanie Tacon*
A Beginners' Guide to Rubber Stamping	*Brenda Hunt*
Blackwork: A New Approach	*Brenda Day*
Celtic Cross Stitch Designs	*Carol Phillipson*
Celtic Knotwork Designs	*Sheila Sturrock*
Celtic Knotwork Handbook	*Sheila Sturrock*
Celtic Spirals and Other Designs	*Sheila Sturrock*

Collage from Seeds, Leaves and Flowers	*Joan Carver*
Complete Pyrography	*Stephen Poole*
Contemporary Smocking	*Dorothea Hall*
Creating Colour with Dylon	*Dylon International*
Creative Doughcraft	*Patricia Hughes*
Creative Embroidery Techniques Using Colour Through Gold	
	Daphne J. Ashby & Jackie Woolsey
The Creative Quilter: Techniques and Projects	*Pauline Brown*
Decorative Beaded Purses	*Enid Taylor*
Designing and Making Cards	*Glennis Gilruth*
Glass Engraving Pattern Book	*John Everett*
Glass Painting	*Emma Sedman*
Handcrafted Rugs	*Sandra Hardy*
How to Arrange Flowers: A Japanese Approach to English Design	
	Taeko Marvelly
How to Make First-Class Cards	*Debbie Brown*
An Introduction to Crewel Embroidery	*Mave Glenny*
Making and Using Working Drawings for Realistic Model Animals	
	Basil F. Fordham
Making Character Bears	*Valerie Tyler*
Making Decorative Screens	*Amanda Howes*
Making Fairies and Fantastical Creatures	*Julie Sharp*
Making Greetings Cards for Beginners	*Pat Sutherland*
Making Hand-Sewn Boxes: Techniques and Projects	*Jackie Woolsey*
Making Knitwear Fit	*Pat Ashforth & Steve Plummer*
Making Mini Cards, Gift Tags & Invitations	*Glennis Gilruth*
Making Soft-Bodied Dough Characters	*Patricia Hughes*
Natural Ideas for Christmas: Fantastic Decorations to Make	
	Josie Cameron-Ashcroft & Carol Cox
Needlepoint: A Foundation Course	*Sandra Hardy*
New Ideas for Crochet: Stylish Projects for the Home	*Darsha Capaldi*
Patchwork for Beginners	*Pauline Brown*
Pyrography Designs	*Norma Gregory*
Pyrography Handbook (Practical Crafts)	*Stephen Poole*
Ribbons and Roses	*Lee Lockheed*
Rose Windows for Quilters	*Angela Besley*
Rubber Stamping with Other Crafts	*Lynne Garner*
Sponge Painting	*Ann Rooney*
Stained Glass: Techniques and Projects	*Mary Shanahan*
Step-by-Step Pyrography Projects for the Solid Point Machine	*Norma Gregory*
Tassel Making for Beginners	*Enid Taylor*
Tatting Collage	*Lindsay Rogers*
Temari: A Traditional Japanese Embroidery Technique	*Margaret Ludlow*
Theatre Models in Paper and Card	*Robert Burgess*
Trip Around the World: 25 Patchwork, Quilting and Appliqué Projects	*Gail Lawther*
Trompe l'Oeil: Techniques and Projects	*Jan Lee Johnson*
Wool Embroidery and Design	*Lee Lockheed*

GARDENING

Auriculas for Everyone: How to Grow and Show Perfect Plants	
	Mary Robinson
Beginners' Guide to Herb Gardening	*Yvonne Cuthbertson*
Bird Boxes and Feeders for the Garden	*Dave Mackenzie*
The Birdwatcher's Garden	*Hazel & Pamela Johnson*
Broad-Leaved Evergreens	*Stephen G. Haw*
Companions to Clematis: Growing Clematis with Other Plants	
	Marigold Badcock
Creating Contrast with Dark Plants	*Freya Martin*

Creating Small Habitats for Wildlife in your Garden   *Josie Briggs*
Gardening with Wild Plants   *Julian Slatcher*
Growing Cacti and Other Succulents in the Conservatory
    and Indoors   *Shirley-Anne Bell*
Growing Cacti and Other Succulents in the Garden   *Shirley Anne Bell*
Hardy Perennials: A Beginner's Guide   *Eric Sawford*
The Living Tropical Greenhouse: Creating a Haven for Butterflies
      John & Maureen Tampion
Orchids are Easy: A Beginner's Guide to their Care and Cultivation
      Tom Gilland
Plant Alert: A Garden Guide for Parents   *Catherine Collins*
Planting Plans for Your Garden   *Jenny Shukman*
Plants that Span the Seasons   *Roger Wilson*
Sink and Container Gardening Using Dwarf Hardy Plants
      Chris & Valerie Wheeler

PHOTOGRAPHY

An Essential Guide to Bird Photography   *Steve Young*
Light in the Landscape: A Photographer's Year   *Peter Watson*

VIDEOS

Drop-in and Pinstuffed Seats   *David James*
Stuffover Upholstery   *David James*
Elliptical Turning   *David Springett*
Woodturning Wizardry   *David Springett*
Turning Between Centres: The Basics   *Dennis White*
Turning Bowls   *Dennis White*
Boxes, Goblets and Screw Threads   *Dennis White*
Novelties and Projects   *Dennis White*
Classic Profiles   *Dennis White*
Twists and Advanced Turning   *Dennis White*
Sharpening the Professional Way   *Jim Kingshott*
Sharpening Turning & Carving Tools   *Jim Kingshott*
Bowl Turning   *John Jordan*
Hollow Turning   *John Jordan*
Woodturning: A Foundation Course   *Keith Rowley*
Carving a Figure: The Female Form   *Ray Gonzalez*
The Router: A Beginner's Guide   *Alan Goodsell*
The Scroll Saw: A Beginner's Guide   *John Burke*

MAGAZINES

WOODTURNING ◆ WOODCARVING ◆ FURNITURE & CABINETMAKING
THE ROUTER ◆ WOODWORKING
THE DOLLS' HOUSE MAGAZINE
WATER GARDENING
OUTDOOR PHOTOGRAPHY ◆ BLACK & WHITE PHOTOGRAPHY
BUSINESSMATTERS

The above represents a full list of all titles currently published or scheduled to be published.
All are available direct from the Publishers or through bookshops, newsagents and specialist retailers.
To place an order, or to obtain a complete catalogue, contact:

GMC Publications,
Castle Place, 166 High Street, Lewes, East Sussex BN7 1XU, United Kingdom
Tel: 01273 488005 Fax: 01273 478606
E-mail: pubs@thegmcgroup.com

Orders by credit card are accepted